ONE MORE TIME 17

A Man's Journey from Alcoholism to Spiritualism

James A. Zimmerman

ISBN 0-7414-3970-0

Published by:

INFIಞITY
PUBLISHING.COM

1094 New DeHaven Street, Suite 100
West Conshohocken, PA 19428-2713
Info@buybooksontheweb.com
www.buybooksontheweb.com
Toll-free (877) BUY BOOK
Local Phone (610) 941-9999
Fax (610) 941-9959

Printed in the United States of America

Printed on Recycled Paper

Published July 2007

Dedication

I would like to dedicate this book to Marge, my wife of 32 years. It is by her inspiration that I have started to write poetry, which is a comfort to the soul. She stayed with me through my many years of alcoholism to live the happier years later. She came to an untimely death at the young age of 52; she fought courageously with her cancer, and continued to stay upbeat until it finally took her life.

I would also like to dedicate this book to my parents and deceased brother; and to Pam, who has shown me that there is yet a life worth living and there will be a brighter tomorrow.

Contents

Chapter 1

My First Alcohol

I had no idea that I could become addicted to alcohol and cigarettes at such a young age. The addictions were easy to come by, but getting rid of them took some hard work, sacrifice, faith, and a lot of support and love from my family and friends. I don't know what it is that makes some of us have addictive personalities, but I sure know that I have one. Having overcome these addictions, I hope I can now help others to do the same. We didn't become addicts in one day, and neither will the addictions go away in one day.

I realized that I had a problem with alcohol several years before I did anything about it. I had to hit what alcoholics call "the bottom" before I dealt with the problem. I think I bounced around on the bottom for quite some time. I tried many different ways to control my drinking, to no avail. Some of the methods seemed to work temporarily, but the outcome was always the same. For me, "one drink for the road" never came — there was always reason for one more.

My first experience with alcohol was when I was about three or four years old. I remember we were visiting relatives, and my parents, aunts, and uncles were drinking a lot of beer. There was a big tub filled with ice and beer, and it was my job to go get them a new beer when theirs were empty. As I walked around the corner of the house by the big shade tree, I realized that one of the bottles still had a little beer left in it. I glanced back to make sure nobody was looking and proceeded to have my first sip of beer. It was warm and bitter, yet somewhat appealing. My brother and the other children were playing with a ball, but I continued to do my job, each time hoping the beer would taste better. It never did get any better. I got sick and dizzy, and swore off drinking for life. I remember lying under the shade tree in pure misery, afraid to tell my parents what I had done.

I didn't drink again for years, and couldn't figure out how anyone could drink alcohol and enjoy it. Then, one day in seventh grade, five of us decided to go into the office and check out of school for the day. Once we were out of school with the whole afternoon to ourselves, we didn't know what to do.

One of the fellows suggested that we go to one of our houses to raid the booze cabinet; I suggested my house, because my parents bought brandy by the case and would not miss a little. We were just into our first drink when the phone rang; we all had a startled look on our faces, as if we knew it was the school calling. It was the principal, who told me to send everyone back to school, including myself. I told him that I would send the others back, but that I really was sick. My parents then wrote a note saying that I hadn't been feeling well, so I got off the hook. My friends each got a week of detention.

I began to drink brandy a couple days a week and enjoyed the buzz I got from it. I found that when I drank I was not quite as shy as I was usually. Liquid courage was a great thing, for the time being. I found out later in life that it was the cause of many problems. One day that winter, a blizzard cancelled school for the day. I drank a little too much, and then proceeded to do my paper route. Between the snow and the alcohol, my bicycle had a hard time staying upright; it was a good thing that the snow provided a soft landing. My paper route took over two hours to complete, compared to the normal 45 minutes.

Once again, I decided that I wouldn't drink alcohol anymore. Much to my amazement, my bicycle learned how to stay on its wheels once more. I did not drink again for about two years; however, I then began to play poker with my paper-route money, and I thought it was cool to smoke while we played cards. While the other guys drank, I stayed sober, and it was easy to win because they played foolishly when they were drinking. I didn't know at the time that I was beginning a pattern of what my life would become.

I attended church and Sunday school and learned of all the evil in the world. I had to test everything on my own, though; my parents tried to teach me right from wrong, but how could they tell me that smoking was bad when they both had a cigarette in their hands? How could they tell me that drinking was bad when they each had a beer or mixed drink in their hand? My parents didn't gamble, however, so I must have picked that up on my own.

I began to like females, but I was much too shy to ask them out. I couldn't figure out how all the other guys got dates and I didn't — and then I remembered the courage that I'd had before after a little to drink. That is when my road to hell truly began.

I was fifteen years old, and had been invited to go to northern Wisconsin for the summer with a friend, to work trimming Christmas trees. John told me that there were all kinds of girls up there, and we would have a great time. We worked ten to twelve hours a day, six days a week, for a dollar an hour without taxes. We had easy access to beer, because some of the people we worked with were old enough to buy it. I remember drinking beer and playing strip poker with some of the local girls. Other than a little hangover here and there, life was great.

Then came my sixteenth birthday, which was to be a real bash. We started out in a pickup truck, with a gallon of vodka and a case of beer; we were going to the stock car races, where it was easy to pick up girls. I remember the terrible noise of the cars going in circles. Beer was flowing all night long, and the cars became more irritating. Back then, the police were quite lenient; I know I didn't look old enough to drink, but they didn't say anything. A young lady took a liking to me and wanted to kiss, but all I wanted to do was throw up. I had drunk way too much again!

The guys I was with knew exactly how to sober me up: they held me up and drove along the old gravel roads. The dust just made me throw up more. I didn't want to quit drinking, but I had to learn how to control it better. Thus began a nineteen-year battle, which I never did win.

Chapter 2

My First Car

I came home from the north woods and it was time to get my driver's license. I passed on the very first try and was given a 1956 Nash Rambler. My nickname was Nim, and my car became known as "Nim's Playpen," because the seats folded down into a bed. It was easy to find female companions when you had a car, especially if you had beer.

My friend John and I were driving around in our hometown one evening when I met Jodi, the first love of my life. I had seen her around town before, but never had the courage to ask her out. Jodi and her friend Lisa were walking home from the library when we stopped the car and asked them if they would like to ride around with us. We had some beer and the two girls were happy to get into the car with us. The only problem was that Jodi liked my friend, and I didn't care for the other girl. At a party a few nights later, John was paying no attention to Jodi, so with the help of my liquid courage, I moved right in. That was the beginning of a rocky three-and-a-half-year relationship.

We dated and thought we had a real love thing going, doing the things that teenagers do and just having fun. Drinking became a major part of our lives, or at least mine. Jodi's parents hated me because I smoked, and they thought I was sneaky, so when prom approached, we pretended to break up. We continued to see each other about three times a week and spent the rest of the time with new friends. We agreed to only kiss our new friends, and break up with them right after prom.

My date, Linda, and I double-dated with a friend of mine and his girlfriend; naturally, we had a case of beer, and I had more in mind than a goodnight kiss. Linda had other ideas, so I dumped her off right after the dance. How could she be that way, after all the money I'd spent on her? Dan and I drove around the countryside drinking beer, until suddenly I saw Jodi parked along a side road with her date. Being drunk, I decided I'd show her. I pushed the gas pedal to the floor as I roared past them.

Dan yelled for me to look out, but it was too late. We were out of road, with nothing but trees in front of us at 100 miles per hour. We crashed, and I remember the horrific noise of the car smashing into a rock pile and the terrible smell from the engine. All I could think was, *Why am I not dead yet?* Dan got out of the car and walked away with the remainder of our case of beer. Bob and Jodi came running up to see how I was. Through some miracle, I had only a scratch on my elbow. I don't know how it happened, but my skid marks headed straight toward the trees when I left the road, and yet my father's car ended up twenty yards to the right of the woods. It was impossible yet it had happened. At that time, I knew that I was saved for some reason; I just didn't know what my purpose in life was yet.

Now I had to go home and tell my dad that I'd just smashed his car beyond repair. My dad was more concerned if I was injured than he was about the car. I don't know if he couldn't smell the beer, or just didn't want to, as parents sometimes don't. Dad had the wrecker come and get the car, and he came home in tears. I felt so bad, because my dad worked two jobs to support us, and that 1960 Chevy was the best car he had ever owned. I told my father that I would quit school and buy him a new car. Dad wouldn't allow that, but I did pay him back later.

That afternoon, the doorbell rang, and there stood a Fond du Lac County policeman. The officer started yelling at me for leaving the scene of an accident, driving too fast for conditions, running a stop sign, and any other charges he could think of. He then accused me of breaking into the beer bar and stealing several cases of beer. After I finally convinced him that I had not been involved in any burglary, he told my dad and me that if I heard who had burglarized the tavern and told him, he would not charge me with anything. At school that Monday, I found out that one of my best friends had been involved in the burglary. I told my dad that I could not snitch on my buddies, and he agreed. Whether he gave the names to the police or not, I won't ever know, but I did not get any tickets, and my buddies all got caught and were forced to join the military after graduation.

A few months later, I got back with Jodi, but it was never the same: in my mind, she had caused my accident. I learned later in life that it is much easier to blame other people for my mistakes than it is to blame myself. This is one of the alcoholic traits that I learned to use so well.

I found a guy who would sell me cases of beer from his tavern if I came out early enough on Friday evenings. I got along well with some of the older guys because I played baseball in league with them. I had quite a nice little side business going. I tried to make about a five-dollar profit on a case of beer. Some Fridays I would have to make two trips to the tavern to haul all the beer.

High school had slipped by so quickly that I didn't realize I might not graduate. The principal called me in and told me there was no way I could finish all of my detentions by graduation time, even if I did have enough credits — which was doubtful — so I decided I would quit school. The principal would not let me, and he took back all of my detentions. I had to do a lot of begging to end up with enough credits to graduate. My parents would be so proud to watch me come down the aisle to get my diploma. My brother had quit school, and I know that hurt them dearly.

I drank my way through school, yet I was going to graduate and go out into the real world. Graduation night was here, and party time was right around the corner. It was a hot night and I stopped at the local tavern to remind my parents what time graduation was. I stumbled as I walked across the stage, and the principal laughed and said someone does it every year. As he handed me my diploma, I glanced through the audience looking for my parents' smiling faces, but I did not see them. I thought that I missed them, so I looked at every face in the audience. They were not there.

I was badly hurt that my parents would choose alcohol over my graduation. Although I was invited to several parties, I got some beer and sat alone drinking. I made a vow to myself that I would never do anything like that to my children. That was a vow I did not keep. I forgive you, Mom and Dad, as I now know what an effect alcohol can have on a person.

Chapter 3

Volunteering For the Army Draft

There I was, out in the real world with no plan for the future. I worked sixty-hour weeks at a gas station for $75. Jodi was trying to figure a budget that we could live on once she graduated and we got engaged. Our relationship was going downhill, though, because I could go to the taverns restricted to 18-year-olds that Wisconsin used to have and she couldn't. I had one-night stands, and I'm sure she did, too.

We broke up and continued to have "one last date." It was only for one thing. We then decided to give it one more try so I got a job at the foundry and I also welded at night to save money for our marriage.

I was welding one night when a friend of mine came into the factory and told me Jodi was at the tavern with another guy. I threw down my welding helmet and went to the tavern to kick some butt. It didn't happen because they were gone already. I got totally drunk and missed work at the foundry the next day. How could she do this to me? In my alcoholic mind, it was okay for me to mess around, but not for her.

We did have a few more "one last" dates, but we both knew it was over. I began fighting a lot and drinking all the more. Most of my money went for alcohol until my dad decided that I should pay room and board. I had no problem with that seeing that there were always meals there when needed, which wasn't too often.

I went to a party one night and Jodi was there with some girls. I had a girl with me, but Jodi kept hitting on me. The more I drank, the more I wanted to be with Jodi. While I was outside watering the grass, I saw Jodi take off with a guy I couldn't stand. Don and I hopped into my 1960 Chevy, just like my dad's old car that I had wrecked, and began to chase them down the winding road along the lakeside. I missed a curve and drove into the lake. The worst part was I had to call the wrecker service that was owned by the father of the guy that was with Jodi.

That was it — now she had caused me to ruin two 1960 Chevrolets! Once again, my alcoholic brain could put the blame elsewhere. I didn't want Jodi, but I didn't want anyone else to have her, either. I was 19 years old with a severe drinking problem. I would come home late at night and drink another six-pack of beer with my mother, who was always ready for one more beer just like me. There was talk that my mother might have an alcohol problem, but back then, no one thought that you could be an alcoholic when you drank just beer most of the time.

When things did not go right, I was angry at the world. I was a drunk and had no way to change my life. The summer of 1967, we drank every night and managed to make it to work about nine out of ten workdays. The hangovers were terrible when working in the hot, noisy foundry. The Vietnam War was going on, and we were starting to worry about the draft. My brother was drafted and had just been sent to Vietnam on his 20th birthday; that really sucked, but he was patriotic and wanted to fight for his country.

In January of 1968, five of us friends were sitting at the tavern talking about the war, and we decided we should all volunteer for the draft. It was much better than enlisting because it was only a two-year duty instead of three. I had taken some tests that would have gotten me a real good job in the Navy, but I figured since I hadn't heard anything from them, I must have flunked the test. The next day all five of us volunteered for the draft.

Shortly before we took off for boot camp, I received a letter from the Navy stating that I had scored quite well on the test and could be accepted for the job. It was too late, though; I was now an Army man.

My brother was wounded in Vietnam and it was time for me to go pay those SOBs back. My friends and I arrived in Fort Campbell in the middle of the night; as soon as we got off the bus, they were yelling at us. Mistake number one was when I smarted off to the sergeant. Once you become known, you are in for eight weeks of hell. My brother had told me to just blend in with the crowd, but it was too late for that. I think my buddy and I set a record for pushups and low crawling in an eight-week period.

My brother had told me to sign up for church each Sunday or I would be put on detail. While marching to church, we took a right and walked right into the canteen, where they had $1 pitchers of beer. With my drinking experience, I had no problem downing two pitchers of beer in one hour. I regretted it later when the drill sergeant unexpectedly stopped in to see us. I had to run around the parking lot for one hour yelling, "I'm a dumb ass; I like to drink beer!" I'd thought it would all change when I got to a new environment, but I still liked to drink too much.

All the extra physical training did help in the long run, because we scored so well on the P.T. test that our whole company was given an overnight pass. Because most of us were only twenty years old, we just got ice and cases of beer, and filled up the bathtub at a motel. I don't remember much about Nashville, except that they have a lot of beer there.

I scored well on a numbers test, so they decided to send me to Artillery Survey School. The day before basic training graduation, we went temporarily AWOL over to the Club 31, which was on base. At 9:55 p.m., while running back to the barracks to make bed check, I tripped and broke my ankle. Alcohol had done me yet another wrong.

Off to Fort Sill I traveled, crutches and all. School was okay because it was quite simple for me; I had never been unintelligent — I just didn't apply myself in school. I ran into one of my high school friends, but he told me he couldn't go out every night and party with me. I guess he wasn't an alcoholic like me. My whole life was centering on alcohol, and I couldn't seem to do anything to stop it.

After I was finished with school, I received a two-week leave to go home and wait on my next orders. It was great; my brother was home from Vietnam, and some other friends of mine were also home on leave. We partied hard for two weeks, not sleeping or eating much. We managed to blow up the engine of the 1966 Oldsmobile Cutlass my brother had purchased. He took it back and was given a 1966 Chevy Malibu to replace it.

I received orders to report to Fort Hood, which was right where my brother was going to finish his time. Brian drove down a week ahead of me, and I flew there to report for duty. Fort Hood was the place where Vietnam returnees served the rest of their time, and it was a holding place for people waiting to go to 'Nam. I was sure that I was going to go to Vietnam, so we had parties every chance we got.

My brother Brian and I would take long weekend drives to the Gulf and party all weekend. On the way back from one of our trips, we met two younger girls who we each began dating. We could only see them on weekends, but we made the best of it. We pretended we were not in the military, but our haircuts gave us away. Both girls' names were Linda, and both of their families were wealthy. We'd drive down to Conroe, Texas, and they would pay for the weekend. The father of the Linda I dated had given her ex-fiancé a used car lot as an engagement present. I really liked her, plus she had money. Our romance ended, however, when my brother broke up with his Linda. My Linda and I wrote a couple of letters more, but our relationship soon ended, too.

Brian and I got into a drunken brawl one night, which left me bitter for years. He told me to quit complaining about the Army and go to Vietnam to do some real Army time. The next day, I volunteered for Vietnam duty. When I called home, my mother was hysterical that I would volunteer to go there. A few weeks later, my orders came for Vietnam and I began my training the next week.

After the first day of training, I received orders to go to Germany. I was then told to report to personnel and find out which orders to follow. The sergeant I spoke with had a 1st Air Calvary patch on his uniform, the same unit my brother went to Vietnam with. He told me you normally follow the last set of orders received, but that he could set it up for me to go whichever place I wanted. I told him that I had volunteered for Vietnam, and that's where I wanted to go. He asked, "Are you nuts? You would rather fight gooks than sleep with the pretty German girls?"

I said, "Send me to Germany."

I was then given a four-week leave, which would have me going to Germany between Christmas and New Year's. It was party time for the next month. A lot of my friends were home for the holidays, and so were the chickens that had gone to college just to avoid the draft. A girl that I knew told me she knew just the right girl for me, a sweet Jewish girl from New Jersey who was going to school in Madison. She was studying to draw cartoons. We had a good couple of weeks together before she headed home for the holidays. She lived in Fort Lee, New Jersey, close to Fort Dix, where I had to report to go overseas.

My brother received an early release from the Army, so he was also home for Christmas. We ironed out our differences somewhat, and Brian was going to take me to the Milwaukee airport so I could fly to New York. A couple days after Christmas, I was on my way to the airport. Freezing rain was falling all across the Midwest and heading east. I told Brian my flight number, and he left on his way home.

I was supposed to fly to Chicago and then on to New York; I was flying military standby, so I had to take what I could get.

At the last minute, they switched airplanes because a seat opened up with a direct flight to New York for me. We took off, and, naturally, I had to have my two little drinks plus a few more for my flight to New York. The stewards were always good to the people in uniform when it came to serving up drinks.

When we got to New York, we could not land because the runways glared with ice. That was okay, because the stewards kept alcohol in front of us. We circled the airport for a couple of hours before we finally landed. I met a Mexican sailor on the flight, and he invited me to go to the tavern with him, his fiancée, and his sister. I called home and my mother was crying. She thought I was dead, because the plane I was supposed to have been on had crashed in Chicago. I had been saved again for some reason.

We partied somewhere in New York until the wee hours of the morning. After I got to Germany and told some of the guys where I had been in New York, they couldn't believe I had gone to that part of town. I actually had left my duffle bag in the doorway, though, and nobody had touched it. Then, I was smashed and on a bus heading to Fort Lee, New Jersey, when all of a sudden, the bus driver told me he was at the end of the line. I was looking for a bus station, but only saw a park bench. I had planned to catch a little sleep in the station, but there wasn't one, so I began to drag my duffle bag on the ice toward a better-lighted area.

The first gas station I stopped at booted me out when I asked if I could take a nap in the corner. The next gas station attendant was much more cordial. When I asked him if he knew where Lemoine Avenue was, he told me I was on it. When I looked across the street, I saw the number 12222; that was where Jan lived. Jan was a girl I had met while home on leave. She was from New Jersey, and was going to college at the University of Wisonsin, Madison. About 4:30 a.m., the young gas station attendant gave me a ride to his basement apartment so I could get some sleep. I was awakened by him and a few girls that wanted to party. I ended up AWOL for a couple days and never did see Jan or remember much ofNew York. I didn't get into any trouble, though, because most of the guys reported for duty late.

A day later, we were on an airplane heading for Germany. I remember it was snowing when we arrived. It reminded me of Wisconsin, and I felt homesick already. Within a day, we were on a little bus headed toward Zirndorf. A couple miles down the road, the German driver offered us a beer for $1; naturally, we all accepted. The beer was warm, bitter, and in a very large bottle. We continued to drink until we came to our destination; then it was time to report for duty. We were all drunk and had to pretend to be sober when we reported to the colonel. He was not fooled at all, and told us to go sleep it off and report for duty in the morning. That was my first drunk spell on German beer, but not my last by far. Most of the guys signed up to learn the German language, but I only wanted to learn how to order a beer. That turned out to be quite easy, because most of the bartenders spoke fluent English.

I was assigned a job as a track driver, which was fun. A track is a vehicle like a tank, but does not have a mounted gun. I got to drive to the country, where we would hook three tracks together with tents as a headquarters for the ranking officers. The only job I had was to put gas in the generator about every two hours. I was always assigned with a lieutenant from Minnesota who liked to drink beer, so when the officers were busy, he would send us to town to get some beer and sausage for a party that night. Some of the parties we had were a little too much to handle. One night, returning to my track to sleep, I fell into the barbed wire that surrounded our camp, and was caught until they cut me loose. Everyone thought it was quite funny, except for me — I was cut and scratched all over. Our field trips were more and more becoming party time as we got to know each other better.

One night after supper, we were told that we were making a night move to a different location. As we were packing, the lieutenant asked me if he could drive the track; I would then be what was called the T.C. man. The T.C. man stood on an adjustable platform, so you could stand up with only your head out of the track. Because of the design of the track, the driver could only see straight ahead and to his left. It was the job of the T.C. man to instruct the driver when he had to move to the right, and did so using wired communication helmets.

This particular move was to take place without any exterior lights on, but we could leave our lights on inside the track because they were not visible outside unless we opened a door. As I was doing my duties, the other man in the track jumped up on the platform, grabbed me around the chest, and began humping me from behind. I was so startled that I just broke free and hit him until he finally struck the door latch. The door flew open and he flew out. It was a good thing that we were traveling with lights off, because when the door flew open, the tank driver behind us saw the interior light in our track and immediately stopped. He was inches from running over the guy's head with his tank. I received verbal counseling for battery to a fellow soldier. I couldn't believe it, but I didn't have much choice in the matter. They told me that if the tank had run over him, I would have been charged with murder. They separated us for the remainder of the exercise and kept him away from me for the rest of my time in Germany.

On another field trip that the lieutenant sent us to town on, we got into trouble. We got lost looking for our campsite, so we continued to drive around in the country and drink beer. We were in a 1 1/4-ton truck with a canvas top; all of a sudden, we saw a convoy of tanks and tracks heading our way. As they passed us, I saw our lieutenant driving my track down the road. We just went to the end of the convoy, turned around, and joined it. We were doing okay at avoiding the brass as we set up camp again until we heard moaning coming out of the back of our truck. Then we remembered that we had picked up a German girl, who got drunk with us and was still in the back of the truck. We somehow convinced her that she had to be quiet and we would get her back to town as soon as possible. A few hours later, we convinced the lieutenant that we needed more beer, so he allowed us to go back to town with the truck. We never did get caught with the female; however, I think the lieutenant knew we had her with us.

I always had my boots well shined and wore neatly pressed clothes, so the first sergeant decided it was time to promote me to sergeant. I had been promoted at Fort Hood, but busted back down because I had got drunk and sunburned all over and refused to drive a five-ton truck. I lost my stripe, and still drove the truck. I decided that I would study really hard to get the stripe and increase in pay. I thought I did very well with the interview, but I never heard any results. Then I accepted a job driving a colonel, which had several perks. I could go right to the front of the chow line to eat, and the colonel set my work hours; most of my duties consisted of driving the colonel to his destination, answering his radio, and keeping his jeep clean. I did so well that I was offered a job driving a two-star general. I turned that job down because I would have been obligated to re-enlist for another year.

The eve of my 21st birthday arrived, and we were ready to celebrate. I decided we should take the colonel's jeep rather than walk; that was absolutely against Army rules, but I saw high-ranking officers take their vehicles out to the bars at night, and I figured they were no better than me. After several beers and some shots of whiskey at the on-base club, I decided it was time to see if we could get off base with the colonel's jeep. The alcohol had once again given me courage that I would not otherwise have possessed.

When we stopped at the gate to go off base, the sergeant recognized the jeep as an officer's and saluted us, and we were on our way. It was kind of neat intermingling with all the brass in town. No one messed with us or asked how we got off base — forbidden for enlisted men. Nobody seemed to care. I let everyone know it was my birthday, and free drinks continued coming my way all night. At closing time, we just drove right back through the gate as if we were high-ranking officers. It was raining quite hard, and I decided to take a shortcut back to our barracks. I drove right across the dirt parade field and watched the mud fly. It was fun for a while, but I figured I had better get back to the barracks to get some sleep, because morning was going to come too soon.

In the morning, I learned the lesson that you do not pick the colonel up in a muddy jeep. I was fired from my job and told to report back to my commander. After a good butt-chewing, I was placed back on regular duty. When our field exercise was completed, we returned to our home base; I was finally given my sergeant stripes, along with orders to go to Vietnam. These orders were soon cancelled, however, because I did not have enough time left in the service.

Alcohol was becoming the main cause of most of my problems. I got into a lot of fights and really didn't care what happened to my life. Each time I went out, I was sure that it would be different and I wouldn't get as drunk. I couldn't figure out how some of the guys could drink a few drinks and then switch to soda. It didn't make any sense to me. Most of the friends I chose, however, drank just like I did; there was no end until closing time, and sometimes later than that. Just about everything I did involved drinking — including going to the zoo, which we got kicked out of for messing with the apes and wild boars. One of the apes sat with his hand nonchalantly behind his back while we mocked him, but then he suddenly threw feces at us. He wasn't as dumb as we'd thought.

After fourteen months of living in Germany, the time came to process out and fly home. I intended to start a new life without all the alcohol. It was much harder than I thought it would be to get out of Germany. One day, as I was going around getting signatures to show I didn't owe any money on post, I told a friend who was getting ready to re-enlist that he would never get post-clearing papers if he re-enlisted. A few minutes later, I was in front of the first sergeant getting my butt chewed again. He was attempting to write me up for conspiracy against the U.S. government and told me I would spend the rest of my life at the Fort Leavenworth jail. I was lucky that the captain liked me and my friend said I'd had nothing to do with talking him out of re-enlisting; I could have faced some pretty ugly charges.

With only days left at one of my last formations, the first sergeant fronted me out, asking if I remembered the little blond girl up the street. He went on to say that she was having a baby and that I was the father. I knew it couldn't be true, because I hadn't been with her for several months after her father escorted me out of the house via shotgun. That had to have been at least ten months previous. It didn't matter, though, as the sergeant took away my clearing papers and told me I would have to stay until tests could prove I wasn't the father. The next day, the black first sergeant laughed as he told me I was free to go: the child had been born, and it was black.

Finally, it was time to get into the back of the truck that was going to take us to the airport. I will never forget the look on the first sergeant's face as I climbed up into the truck. I did not say a word as I boarded and I didn't look back, in fear that the sergeant would find some reason to keep me there.

It was nice arriving back in the States, the service behind me. I met a friend at the airport who was also traveling to Fort Dix to process out of the Army. Tom was a stocky guy, a catcher for a Chicago Cubs farm club. As we were walking out of the bus terminal to hail a taxi, we realized we were about to be robbed by six young black kids with knives. We looked back; three more kids with knives stood behind us. I wasn't used to this — having been raised in a small Wisconsin town — and I was filled with fear.

Before I could decide what to do, Tom said, "Follow me," and he swung his duffle bag in front of him and ran right at the six knife-wielding little thugs. He mowed them over like a corn picker would mow a row of corn. Before I knew it, we were out on the street climbing into a cab. The next morning, we processed out and were on our way home.

We got drunk at the airport while waiting for our flight, which was running late due to a snowstorm. By the time we finally boarded the plane, I was in need of a nap from my alcohol consumption. I woke up and panicked when I realized I was the only person left on the plane. As I jumped up, a stewardess told me that we were laid over in Detroit due to the storm. What a relief that was, because I thought I had slept through Milwaukee and that we were in Minnesota.

It was such a great feeling to land in Milwaukee and be greeted by my father. Something was wrong, though, because my mother was not with my father, and I knew that after being gone for fourteen months she would want to see me. My dad said that my mother's emphysema was getting worse; she was still smoking. I decided that I would quit smoking and learn to drink in moderation.

Chapter 4

A New Life

There I was with the Army behind me and the rest of my life ahead of me. After spending some time with my family, I had my dad take me to the bar to see if any of my friends were there. They were all back from the Army, and it was just like old times. Some of them had changed and were heavy into smoking pot and other drugs. I had tried pot in the Army, but was not too attracted to it because it made me hungry and lazy. We partied for a couple days while I decided what I wanted to do with my life.

I went back to work at the foundry because I really didn't know what I wanted to do. I had saved enough money in the Army for a down payment on a 1967 Pontiac GTO. How I didn't get killed in that car, I'll never know. I didn't know it at the time of purchase, but that car had an experimental engine in it and it was extremely fast. I would drag race with my friends who had brand new 396 Chevrolets and fly right by them.

One night, I bet a guy that we could make it back to the minor bar — seventeen miles away — in fifteen minutes, including going through a town. As I came around the last curve before a seven-mile straightaway, I pressed the gas pedal to the floor. I was doing 115 miles per hour when I shifted into fourth gear, and when I looked in my rearview mirror, I saw a faint red light way behind me. When I reached the edge of town, my radiator was steaming, so I stopped at a gas station to add some water.

As I opened the hood of my car, a Waupun Police car pulled up behind me. I recognized the cop as my neighbor. He asked, "What in the hell are you doing?" He went on to say he had been going to the edge of town to set up a roadblock for me. I then looked up the street and saw a Dodge County cop with his lights flashing and siren blaring. I had to really do some smooth talking to get out of that one. I told him I had just gotten out of the Army, and had gone to see my girlfriend and caught her with another guy. My neighbor verified that I had just been in the Army, and the county cop let me go with just a butt chewing. Back in the early 1970s, the police were quite lenient with drinking and driving.

I tried to control my drinking, but nothing worked. I wanted to find a girlfriend, settle down, and eventually get married, but all I seemed to find were one-night stands. Then, one night when I was outside the minor bar talking to my friend's girlfriend, a young lady walked by; I was totally attracted to her. I told Cheri that I had to have that girl; she had no interest in me, however.

A few weeks later, Jane, a mutual friend, talked Marge into going out with me. We went to the county fair, and I spent my whole paycheck winning her stuffed animals and trying to impress her. When I took her home, she wouldn't even give me a goodnight kiss. She was nothing like the girls I was used to taking out. She later said she was afraid of me because of the stories she had heard. I was convinced that she was the lady for me, but I didn't really know how to win her over. We started dating, and finally I got a kiss from her.

One night, we were at a party where Marge and her friends lived. I became very upset when I thought Marge was spending too much time talking to one guy who had not brought a date. In my anger, I jumped into my GTO and sped off. After almost crashing several times, I went back to my hometown. When I woke up the next morning and remembered what I had done, I called to apologize, but Marge was not home. I continued to call all day long, until I realized that she was with the guy from the previous night. I then went out and got drunk all over again, thinking that would help things.

I was now working for a tree-trimming company, and had to drive 100 miles the next day and then work for ten hours. It was a terrible day for me, thinking I had lost my girlfriend and feeling sorry for myself. That night, I drove 100 miles back to town just to talk to Marge, but she was not there. That was one of the longest weeks of my life, waiting to return home to talk to Marge and try to straighten things out. I knew I couldn't live without her. We did get back together, but I know she didn't like my temper and I vowed to myself that I would work on trying to change it, along with my drinking habits.

My mother's health was worsening, but she didn't quit smoking. I couldn't figure how she could continue to smoke with her breathing being so difficult. I would sit up at night with my mother on the weekends, drinking beer and smoking cigarettes while pleading with her to quit smoking. On many occasions, I can remember my father yelling at us to go to bed. A few times, he did get up and have a few beers with us, but I think that was just to get rid of the beer so we would go to bed.

After several months of dating and several arguments with Marge, I didn't know what to do to make our relationship better. One night, I discussed our relationship with Marge's friend Jane, who suggested I present Marge with an engagement ring. I'll never forget the night I gave Marge the engagement ring, because after she accepted and we got to her apartment, she told me to leave. I didn't know if she was happy or having second thoughts, but for me it was a good reason to celebrate.

Meeting My Wife

Like a slow, cool breeze you drifted into my life
From that moment on, I knew I wanted to make you my wife
I saw your smile and hoped it wasn't a tease
After a few dates, my mind was at ease
The time to pose the question was getting near
Would you accept the ring, no reason to fear
With grateful acceptance, I slid on the ring
We were both happy, we had reason to sing
Soon we got married to show our love
My mother had passed, so she watched from above

We set the wedding date for about a year later. I figured that if I was going to get married and raise a family, it was time to get rid of the GTO and get a smaller family car. I traded for a 1970 Ford Maverick, which lasted a couple months before the transmission went out. When I told the salesman about the piece of junk he'd sold me, he said I had bought the car "as-is." A few days later, the salesman called me to ask where the spare tire from the GTO was; I told him that we had traded as-is. The rims on the GTO were special, so I sold him the rim and spare tire for $135. I then bought a 1967 Pontiac Lemans that would become our family car.

After a softball team party in the summer of 1971, I decided to drive Marge back to Fond du Lac following a whole afternoon and evening spent drinking beer. I made it about five miles before I fell asleep and drove off the road, causing severe damage to my car. Neither Marge nor I were injured. It was the third time I had an alcohol-related car accident with no injuries. I knew I had to stop drinking in excess, but

I wanted to be able to drink moderately; I felt there had to be a way for me to learn how to drink responsibly, because I couldn't be an alcoholic at the age of 23. Due to the fact that my dad knew a Fond du Lac County police officer, I got away without a ticket again.

The Christmas season of 1971 was not very happy, because my mother had become sicker; shortly after New Year's, she was admitted to the hospital and hooked up to a breathing machine. A short time later, she was given a tracheotomy so that she could get air. I knew my mother's condition was growing worse, and I wanted to be by her side, but that was impossible because I was trimming trees ninety miles away.

I asked my boss if I could have off for a few days to be with my mother; he said no, but that I could call her whenever possible. I told him to stick the job, and so did one of the other trimmers; down the road we went. I got home shortly before noon and went directly to the hospital. When I walked into my mother's room, I discovered that the air tube into her throat had come out. She was clutching at the call button with both her hands, but nobody was coming to help her.

I ran to the nurses' station and told the nurse that my mother needed help *now*. She told me that my mother was not the only person in the hospital who needed help. She also told me she would get there when she had time. I then told her to get her ass down to my mother's room now because it was urgent, and finally she responded. Once she saw what had happened, she was very apologetic; I called my father, however, and we had Mom transported to a different hospital. In the thirty years since then, I have only used that hospital on one extreme emergency, and then with unpleasant results.

It was terrible watching my mother, helpless and with machines keeping her alive. I literally spent days in the hospital by my mother's side. She knew I was there; I felt her squeeze my hand a couple of times. On January 24, 1972, at 11:10 p.m., my mother passed away from complications of years of smoking. I decided that I would never smoke again; I did not want to go through what my mother had just gone through. I was very sad because my mother would not be around for our wedding, which she had been looking forward to so much. My mother was only 49 years old, but would never have a chance to be a grandmother to my children.

My father and I both quit smoking for about a week, but both started up again because of the stress in our lives. I was getting married in a few months and did not have a job. In April of 1972, I applied for a job in a state mental hospital, which also housed some state inmates. I had a very easy interview with a man that my father knew, and was hired on the spot.

That evening I went out to celebrate my new job, and a friend of mine came to the tavern looking for me. He told me that his pipeline crew was looking for a laborer and the pay would be much better than what the state paid. I decided that I would work for the pipeline, and went to talk to the pipeline foreman. Dick told me that I should trim my mustache because the foreman didn't like facial hair. Back in 1972, bosses could control their workers' appearances somewhat, but I don't think that Jerry even looked at my mustache, and he hired me on the spot. I called the man that had hired me for the state and told him I had accepted another job.

I found pipeline work to be very physical; I liked that, because I wanted to stay in shape. Also, every night after work, someone would buy a twelve-pack of beer for the ride home, and a lot of nights we would also stop at the tavern. We felt we deserved some beers after a hard day of work.

My wedding day was fast approaching. We decided we would live with my father for a while until we were a little more financially fit. We also felt that my father needed some company since he had just lost his wife. The last few weeks before our wedding, I did a lot of partying while Marge did a lot of the final planning. A couple of weeks before the wedding, I gave a girl a ride home from a party after the bar's closing time. After dropping her off at her house, I fell asleep on a curve and drove my car into a deep ditch. This was the fourth alcohol-related car crash I had been in with no injuries. I still didn't realize that most of my problems were related to alcohol. Yet again, because the county policeman knew my father I did not get a ticket; by the ripe age of 23, I could have had four drunk driving tickets if the circumstances had been different. I was so lucky that my accidents did not involve other vehicles, because I could have easily killed someone or injured them badly. Due to some quick work by my friends at the body shop, my car would be fixed and ready for my wedding.

Chapter 5

Getting Married

The night before my wedding, several friends and my brother took me out for one final drunk as a single person. I felt so bad in the morning that I didn't even want to get up to get married, but I arrived at the church in plenty of time to drink the glass of wine the priest gave me to settle my nerves. The wedding went quickly, and then it was time for the reception. My brother had told me to stay sober for my wedding, so I thought I would try to do that. He told me to walk around with half a beer and people wouldn't bother me to drink; that worked quite well, and I didn't get real drunk on my wedding night. That was May 13, 1972, and today is May 13, 2002: thirty years that I have been married to the wonderful lady who once was so afraid of me.

We bought the beer for the wedding from the tavern where I worked part-time, so we got a good deal on six half-barrels of beer. I don't know where everyone put it, but all six half-barrels were polished off that night. One of Marge's uncles who had been sober for a few years got drunk and began arguing with one of my friends about cars. I talked him into going back inside, and naturally, he headed right to the bar, where the twin brother of the guy he had been arguing with was bartending. It was hilarious watching the expression on his face; he began to argue with Tom exactly where he'd left off with Jerry. Tom did not have a clue what he was talking about, so finally I told Ed that he was talking to Jerry's twin brother.

We were married about thirty miles from my hometown, and it is very scary to think back about all the intoxicated people who drove home that night. Some of the smarter guests got motel rooms, but there were quite a few driving home.

Marge and I took what we called a pipeliner's honeymoon, staying in a motel overnight, opening gifts the next day, and returning to work on Monday. We had already moved into my father's house, so there wasn't any moving to do. I think my father was quite happy to have us around, and he cooked most of our dinners because Marge and I worked later than he did. My job required me to work some places that were much too far to drive to every day, so we stayed in motel rooms or cottages when on the road. There wasn't much to do except lay around in the motel or go to the bar at night, so most of us chose to drink many nights of the week.

During the summer months, I played softball on weekends and any of the other games I could make. Naturally, it was always party time after our games, and most of the times I went without my wife. I had thought that my drinking habits would change with marriage, but they seemed to get worse. I bought a brand new, 15-foot fiberglass boat, and I figured that my drinking would slow down if I went fishing a lot. I did fish a lot, but there was always room for a big cooler full of beer in the boat. The very first time we took my boat out on the water, we took two cases of beer with us. My brother and another guy each got so drunk that they dove into the water while the boat was going thirty miles an hour. They dove into three feet of water; luckily, neither of them was hurt.

In the fall of 1972, I was working in Milwaukee, putting in a jet fuel line at Billy Mitchell Field. I was off on Sunday, November 5th, and my brother, Brian, was coming up from Madison to do some pheasant hunting. He and his wife were separated, and he had custody of his three-year-old son that day. My sister and my wife agreed to watch Brian's son while we went hunting. We hunted most of the morning and part of the afternoon, before deciding to go to the tavern to play pool. We drank some beer and played pool until about seven that evening, when my brother ran out of money. We had not had the best relationship as brothers but I told him I would lend him $20. As I handed him the money, he hugged me and said, "Hey, we are truly brothers."

We left the tavern about 8 p.m., because Brian had to pick his son up and take him back to his mother's house by 9 p.m. When we picked up Brian's son, Marge and Donna told Brian that his son was not feeling well, and that he should tell his ex-wife to take him to the doctor to have him checked out. Brian, his son, I, and two other friends then drove Brian's son to his in-laws' house, arriving about 8:50 p.m.

I could hear Brian and his ex-wife arguing, so I went to the doorway inside the garage and beckoned to Brian to leave. I knew Brian had a temper, and I just wanted to get him out of there before trouble started. I walked through the open door into a hallway that led to the kitchen area. When Brian walked out the door, it slammed closed in my face.

At that time, as I reached to open the door, Brian's ex-mother-in-law began slapping me in the face, saying, "You f—ing Zimmermans are all alike. You are all no good!" I felt the door open, and saw Brian run into the kitchen at his ex-father-in-law, who had a gun pointed at me. The man hit Brian in the head with the .22-caliber rifle's stock, knocking him to the ground. I shoved the ex-mother-in-law against the wall and ran into the kitchen to help Brian up. I then heard the ex-father-in-law yell to his minor son, "Shoot him!"

As the gun exploded, I felt Brian jerk from my grip and slump to the floor. There wasn't much blood, but there was a gaping hole in my brother's stomach. Brian looked at me with fear in his eyes and said, "I'm hit; I'm dying. The bastard killed me." Those were the last words I ever heard my brother say.

The minor son then said to me, "That was meant for you; you shoved my mother." He then banged his head on the doorjamb causing blood to gush from his eye area. Little chance did my brother have of surviving a 12-gauge shotgun blast at close range, but I ran to the phone to call an ambulance, only to be blocked by Brian's ex. Dave and Phil came running into the house when they heard the gun blast; Dave told the kid to put the gun down, which he did. They also put aside the .22-caliber rifle, which now had a cracked stock from hitting Brian's head.

I ran out of the house, drove to a neighbor's, and called the ambulance and also the sheriff's department. The sheriff's department dispatcher told me that an accidental shooting had been reported at that address a few minutes earlier. I told her that no, it had not been accidental at all. We then drove back to the house and met the ambulance and squad cars as they arrived. My brother was pronounced dead on arrival at the hospital. Dave, Phil, and I were each put in separate squad cars to give our statements, while the minor and his family got into the sheriff's car to give a statement.

We were then taken to the sheriff's department, where the sheriff told me my brother was dead. I called my wife and had her come pick me up. When we arrived home, my dad walked into the house smiling. His smile quickly disappeared when I told him his oldest son had just been shot to death. When I told him who had done it, my father said, "Then he must die, too." My father did not own any guns, and wanted one of mine to go kill the minor; he felt he had nothing to live for after losing a wife and a son in the same year. Of course, I did not give him a gun, because I knew the minor would be punished severely — or at least I thought so at the time.

The next day, the local radio station made it sound like we had broken into the house and that they were justified in shooting my brother. I called the radio station and told them they were reporting a totally incorrect story. They never changed it, however, and it was heard every half an hour or so, making our family name sound bad. At the funeral home, someone told me that my brother looked good. I remember telling him, "No, he looks dead, and they will pay for it."

Those were some of the saddest days in my life, as I felt partially to blame because my brother had come back into the house to help me. He had sacrificed his life so I could live! The day before the funeral, my uncle was over and wanted to know exactly what had happened. I told the story as we sat and drank shot after shot of whiskey to ease the pain. I couldn't understand how anyone could pull a trigger and end a person's life. I drank until I couldn't drink any more, and then went to bed. Nothing had changed by morning. It wasn't a dream; it was a reality, and we had to deal with it.

We had a military funeral for Brian, and when they did the 21-gun salute, I just shuddered. The gun sounds were too familiar in my mind; I thought I was going to pass out, but I didn't. I wasn't told then, but the father of the minor was at the cemetery when Brian was buried. I was glad that nobody told me at the time, because I'm not sure what I would have done.

Chapter 6

The Coroner's Inquest

It was November of 1972, and I had lost my mother to emphysema and my brother to a gunshot wound. I was totally confused, and didn't understand how a loving God could do this to our family. I quit going to church because I no longer believed in God — why waste my time on it?

I found out that there were going to be no charges filed against the kid who shot my brother. I could not believe it. The only chance we had of seeing any justice was that there was a coroner's inquest into the matter, to see if there was reason to bring charges against the family. As far as I was concerned, they had all helped kill my brother and they all should be punished.

Brian had a female divorce attorney who was very interested in the inquiry, and she called me to discuss the matter. We didn't have money to hire an attorney to make sure the inquiry was legitimate, but Ann volunteered her time because she didn't like the way that the newspaper was writing everything up. She talked to me to get my side of the story, and she was well satisfied that I was telling the truth — which I was. I never expected people to tell anything but the truth, but I sure had been wrong there. After I'd talked to Ann a couple of times, she told me that she knew I was telling the truth, and I asked her how she could tell that. She told me it was because I was so consistent with my story. She said people who lie keep changing their stories to make them sound better.

Ann met me at the courthouse and talked to me the day of the inquiry, saying that I was the only one who could convince the jury that a murder had taken place. I knew I didn't have much of a chance to convince the jury, because they had been hand selected by the sheriff, and he was good friends with the family that killed my brother. It was the most helpless feeling I have ever had. I took the stand and told the truth from beginning to end. I then sat and listened to all the family members tell lie after lie to cover their butts. I feel for anyone that has ever been done an injustice by the judicial system. I could see it coming that I would leave the building very unhappy. Why would a hand-picked jury of friends find reason to send a teenager to trial for murder? I will never forget how they portrayed my brother to be the size of a large football player. My brother was 5 feet, 9 1/2 inches tall and weighed 165 pounds. Not too many football players are that small.

They said the shot had been fired because they feared for their lives. I still don't know what it was that they were afraid of. Brian was out of the house and came back in only when he saw a gun pointed at me.

After a short period of deliberation, the jury came out and found — as had been expected by Ann and myself — that there was no reason for a trial. Prior to the inquiry, my father and I had talked to the juvenile prosecutor from that county, and he told us he wouldn't prosecute because he didn't want to chance ruining his 100% conviction rate for juvenile homicides. I was so angry that I felt like going over the desk and teaching him how victims felt. I could not believe my ears, but by the time the case went to the inquiry, I pretty much knew the outcome would be unfavorable, and it was.

As unbelievable as it was, I had to learn to live with the outcome of the inquiry. Afterwards, I felt I needed to drink to go on with life. It was the perfect excuse for the alcoholic I already was. Day after day, I drank; everyone felt it was appropriate for me to be smashed every day, considering what I had been through.

Marge did all she could to comfort me, for which I am still grateful. It took a very special person to stay with me during that time. I wanted to go kill the whole family of the juvenile that killed Brian, and felt I would be justified in doing so. I was lucky that Marge called the police on me one night, or I might have done it. I was lucky and got pulled over by a policeman that had believed my side of the story and sent me home. When he stopped me, I had three loaded weapons in my car and I meant business. I am so happy I never carried out any of my drunken thoughts, even though I felt they would have been justified because the whole family had lied at the inquiry.

It is very hard to put your brother in the ground and watch the person who pulled the trigger get nothing out of it. Even being a drinker, I always believed in honesty, a trait that the other people didn't seem to have.

Chapter 7

Dealing with Alcohol

As much as I was in disbelief about what all had happened in 1972, I was just recently married and had a life to get on with. Marge was very comforting and did all she could to help me deal with the grief. However, each day I couldn't handle it, and ended up getting drunk most days. I didn't want my life to go the way it was going but I couldn't stop. I tried all different ways of trying to control my drinking, but I still got drunk. For a while, I tried a few shots and then soda, but I got drunker; I tried not drinking until after supper, but then we couldn't stop after work. Of course, I felt I had to drink after work with the guys. The only difference was most of those guys went home after a few drinks, but I continued drinking until late at night. I had so many rough days at work that I swore off drinking just about every time I got drunk. It was a continual cycle that I was going through, and as much as I wanted it to stop, it just got worse.

One night after work when I was halfway sober, Marge told me she was pregnant. We were both so happy, and I thought that a baby in the house would help me to stop drinking. I will never forget how proudly Marge walked while she was carrying our first child. She was due to have the baby around Christmas, and we couldn't wait. I tried everything I could without giving up alcohol completely, but nothing worked. Marge was quite large in the stomach area and we thought she would give birth earlier, but it wasn't to be.

It was the night before Christmas Eve; as we were sitting at home, Marge told me to go get her a pair of underwear because her water had broken. I had been drinking, and so I came back downstairs with a pair of my underwear. Once we finally got Marge cleaned up and ready to go, I was speeding very fast through town, and Marge had to tell me to slow down, which I did. I had gone to the classes and was going to go in and watch our child be born. That didn't happen, however, as the nurse smelled my breath and escorted me to the waiting area. I passed out and slept most of the night away. I woke up shaking the doctor's hand. He told me everything had gone well, and we had a big healthy boy. I was so happy and swore after the celebration that I would quit drinking and become a responsible parent. Marge was so happy; I can still remember the smile on her face as I entered the room to meet our baby. I just knew my life would change now that we had a child.

I went out drinking and told Marge I would come back to see her later, which I did; however, I was quite intoxicated when I got back. I couldn't believe the number of people that were out drinking already the morning of Christmas Eve. I called all my relatives and friends and a lot of them came out to celebrate with me. When I got back to the hospital to visit Marge, I was drunk once again. I didn't want to be, but I was. Freezing rain was falling outside and Marge didn't want me out driving, but I was determined to drive 33 miles to my father and stepmother's house. My guardian angels had to have been with me that night, or I wouldn't be here writing this book. Somehow, I made it, and the shots of brandy started rolling. I don't remember passing out, but I did, which was a good thing.

When I woke up to drive home, I was sick and felt like I wanted to die. Again I swore off drinking; it lasted for a day. I knew I had a problem and I wanted it to go away, but it wouldn't. I tried my best to be a good father, but day after day, I continued to drink to excess. I was off for the winter and spent a lot of my time at the bars. I would start out with good intentions, but always ended up getting drunk. I could go two or three days without alcohol, but then when I went out, I made up for the lost days. I know I acted like a fool and there were times when Marge didn't want me to hold Brian when I had been drinking. As I drank, I began to gamble a little more heavily than I had been. We used to shake dice for drinks, but now I was shaking dice for dollars. I really didn't have money to be gambling with.

When I went back to work in the spring, I could drink when we were working out of town and nobody would bother me about it. I tried to stay sober on weekends when I came home, and sometimes it worked. But then there were Friday nights that I would take Marge out for a fish fry; they were like a free night of drinking where Marge wouldn't get mad at me. I was starting to act more and more like a fool each time I got drunk. I didn't pick fights, but if anyone as much as looked at me wrong, it was fighting time.

Alcoholism

Alcoholism is a disease of progression

You hope and pray it will go into recession

I ran and ran and didn't make any gain

I ran for change, but it stayed the same

I feel like I'm on a merry-go-round

I want to stop and put my feet on the ground

I try and try, I want to quit

But my head tells me I can have a little bit

I go out and try to keep my drinking under control

But before I know it, I'm again on a roll

Each day I say I'll never drink anymore

Each day ends up like the day before

I look at my wife and can see her pain

I want to quit and make her happy again

My life continued on a downward spiral, drinking most evenings and trying to keep our marriage together at the same time. It was a little better if I took Marge out with me, because she didn't try to control my drinking if she knew she could drive home. I think she just hoped that some day I would get my fill of alcohol, but that didn't happen, and as hard as I tried, the progression of the alcoholism got worse. It was as though someone had a tight grip on me and made me drink. There were also days when I thought I couldn't be an alcoholic because I didn't drink every day; I drank most of them, but not every one. I also thought I couldn't be an alcoholic because I only drank beer.

It was early 1976, and Marge was pregnant again. I thought maybe after this child came, it would be more responsibility and I could become sober. In my mind, I felt that I could continue to drink until the new baby was born, and then I would quit. It seemed reasonable to me, but deep down I knew it wouldn't happen. I think Marge just condoned it because she came from a strict Catholic family, and they didn't believe in divorce.

That year, we worked a lot of jobs too far away to come home at night, so no one knew how much I drank but me. When I would come home on the weekends, I would have to go out to meet my friends. Sometimes Marge would come along, and sometimes I would go out myself. There were times that I couldn't remember coming home at night or how I got there. There were times that I would look out the window and my truck would be nowhere in sight, and I didn't have any idea where it was. I was sick of hangovers, but didn't know how to quit. Each time I tried, it just snuck up on me again.

Growing With Alcohol

As I grew older, I seemed to know
The direction I was heading spelled trouble

I drank a lot and didn't have a care

I had lost my self-esteem long ago, it was no longer there

When I drove, I was reckless as heck

I didn't care until I had another wreck

Each accident I had I swore I would change

But my thoughts and habits I couldn't rearrange

I quit many times and I was convinced I knew

That I could go out and have just one or two

It did not work, I'd go home thinking I tried

I would look at my wife and know she had cried

Alcohol kept getting a tighter grip on me

I begged let me go, just set me free

Marge called the hotel I was staying at and told me she had reported to the hospital to give birth to our second child. I was drunk again. I started to drive the 100 miles home. I now hate the thought of people like I used to be out on the road at night, driving while intoxicated. When I arrived at the hospital it was around 6 a.m., and Marge's friend, Jane, hollered out the window, "It's a boy!" I was happy even though we did want to have a girl.

After spending a couple hours with Marge, it was time to go buy cigars and celebrate. It was pretty early in the morning to celebrate, but my friend at the auto body repair shop was ready to drink with me. After we drank our first twelve-pack, a couple more friends came and we got some more beer. It was already late in the afternoon of November 3, 1976, and I realized I should go to visit Marge again. All I could think about was that it was two days prior to the day my brother had been shot and killed in 1972. After I visited Marge for a while, I drank until the wee hours of the morning. November

4th, I was too sick to think about drinking and I stayed sober all day, but I was hurting and I again swore off drinking for good.

I felt pretty good the next morning, November 5th, when I picked Marge and our new baby, Tim, up at the hospital. After bringing them home, I realized that it was exactly four years ago that my brother had been killed. I went out to alleviate the pain of his loss by consuming large amounts of beer and brandy. I don't remember going home that night, but I'm sure I made quite an impression on my wife and my in-laws, who had been watching Brian while Marge was in the hospital. The cycle continued. I would get so drunk that I would quit for a day or so, and it would be right back to the beer a day later when I didn't feel as bad.

More Alcohol

I wondered how Marge put up with me for all of those years

I know she had shed so many tears

Broken promises were becoming my way

They were happening more often, almost every day

I didn't know how or when I could stop this behavior

I knew somewhere out there, there must be a savior

I always had money to go out on the town

*When Marge needed money for the children,
she was met by my frown*

I was beginning to see how my life would be

If by some chance I didn't find total sobriety

I tried to quit drinking now that I had two children and a wife to support, but soon my body became victim as I was again drinking. I tried to control my every urge, but I just couldn't do it and I gave in each time. I tried to go home earlier, but that only worked for a few nights and then I was back to normal. I just couldn't figure out how alcohol had such a tight grip on me and everything I did. I talked to people that had sobered up, but it didn't seem like their way was for me. After all, I no longer believed in God, so how could I go along with some twelve-step program?

I watched as friends of mine became sober and appeared to have happy lives. Some of them had lost jobs, some had gotten divorced, and some had lost about everything. They all seemed to be bringing their lives back together, but I decided I wasn't ready for that yet. I didn't drink every day and I had a good excuse to be angry at the world: my mother had died and my brother was killed in the same year. It just wasn't fair, and I felt it gave me a reason to walk around angry and drink all I wanted.

My drinking was starting to cause more arguments at home, and when I got angry, I just went out and got drunk. I got to a point that I was happy to work out of town so I didn't have to listen to the lectures about my drinking. One time, I didn't drink for seven days, and everyone thought I had died or something. The language I used around my wife and children was unacceptable and I feel bad about it now. A lot of our arguments started about money. I didn't have money to buy the children new shoes, but I had money to go out and drink.

I was asked at work if I wanted to switch crews and work on a crew that normally stayed closer to home. I did it in hopes that being closer to my house; I would go home after work instead of going to the bar. A few nights it worked, but then I discovered most of this crew liked to drink just like I did. We finally got a job in my hometown. I thought I would be home early every night and be able to take my children and wife to the park and fishing and do other normal things that parents do. It didn't work out that way, though. We drank beer down by where we parked our equipment each night, and I still went home drunk. I was really becoming sick of my behavior, but kept thinking each day that it would change and I would only drink a couple cans of beer and then go home. A couple times, I did do that, but it just didn't seem normal and I would end up going downtown with some friends and finishing off my drunk.

Even though we argued and Marge was upset with me, she very seldom raised her voice to me. She showed how hurt she was, and in my drunken state, I verbally abused her quite often. I didn't really mean anything by it, but later I realized how I had hurt her verbally. After more than twenty years of sobriety, I still feel bad for my past actions. Marge was such a sweet person, and I didn't realize how good I had it. Even when I was drunk, she always tried to please me. That is just the type of person she was. I am so grateful I got to spend so many years with her, twenty of them sober.

On the weekends, we would go camping with my sister and brother-in-law. He liked to drink like I did, but at least we didn't have to drive unless we ran out of beer. We had a lot of fun sitting around the campfire and telling stories and, of course, drinking. Marge and my sister would drink once in a while too, which made for a fun night. I always hated having to drive home on Sunday afternoon with the thought of work the next day.

We could bring Brian and Tim along; there was a swimming pool and other things for them to do as well. I remember how one night a drunk kid was speeding around the campground, and instead of just turning him in to the campground owners, I stopped him and pulled him out of his car and threw him down. I was a big hero to all the campers with children, which really pumped up my ego. We also could bring my boat along and take our children fishing, which they enjoyed at their young age. It was almost like being a regular family, except for the excessive alcohol consumption.

As shy as Marge had been for years, her bikini bathing suit was not the conservative type she used to wear. She was a beautiful young lady, and I was very protective of her and also very jealous — another alcoholic tendency. We were so much in love, but I just couldn't kick the alcohol. I didn't know how life could go on without alcohol. I thought people who didn't drink were all geeks, and I didn't want to be that way.

I was caught in a state of confusion, as I wanted to quit drinking, yet I loved the feeling I got from getting drunk. I kept trying to slow down, but there was no such thing as cutting back. You can ask any recovering alcoholic and they will all tell you of the dozens of times they tried to cut back to no avail.

I had started hunting now, and in the fall months, when I was working close enough to home, I would go deer hunting with my bow and arrows. I was not a very good shot: I always took beer into the tree stand with me, and was not too steady by the time deer would come by. I missed a lot of shots and always had an excuse. This is a great alcoholic characteristic, blaming everything and everyone else for my faults.

Gun season was just another big drunk. My friend had a big remodeled school bus that would sleep about ten of us, so we would drive up to northern Wisconsin for opening day of gun season. I very seldom saw any deer because I was half-asleep from my hangover. When I look back, it is amazing how many deer I have shot since I became sober compared to when I was drinking. When we went up North for our hunt, we would drink all the way up there in the bus, which I think was legal as long as the driver wasn't drinking. This drive up North for the gun hunt became our tradition for several years. We had a lot of fun and never hurt the deer population in northern Wisconsin.

Chapter 8

Losing My Job

I had managed somehow to stay married for nine years. I was asked if I wanted to go out of state and work for the summer and fall. After talking it over, we decided that I would go because I could make a lot of money, which we needed to help bring up our children and for things around the house. We had bought our house from my father, and were slowly trying to fix it up. Before I went to work in South Dakota, I was told that we would work a lot of hours and bank them up so we could come home for four or five days every three weeks. It sounded pretty good, but things didn't happen that way at all. The first time we got to come home was after we had been working out there for five weeks; then, we drove home on a Friday morning and had to be back to work by Monday morning.

House and a Home

We wanted a home with children and a white picket fence

That's not much too ask for, just common sense

What I had wanted all of my life

I was granted by God with my beautiful wife

She had long, brownish hair and a wonderful smile

I knew I would love her for a very long while

After our wedding, we lived with my dad

He had lost his wife and was feeling quite bad

Marge and I both worked into the early night
When we got home, the table was set, much to our delight
We bought Dad's house and made it a home
This would be the place our children would become grown
We lived in our home for over 32 years
Until God took Marge away and brought on the tears

I was getting sick of all the lies I was hearing from my employer, telling us we would be able to go home more often, but that day just didn't come on time. I was getting sick of being away from my family and wanted to be back home, but I continued to work long hours to try to get ahead financially. I was kind of running the crew when the boss was out looking ahead for our next day's work. The guys liked working for me because I didn't yell at them without a reason as our boss did. I had been promised a foreman's job earlier in the summer and realized I sure could use the extra money.

I was beginning to see a pattern in my life, which kind of startled me. When I was in the Army, I had promoted right up the ladder and was actually a rank higher than I should have been for the amount of time I had been in the Army. I was also promised another stripe if I re-enlisted for a few more years. When I quit my tree-trimming job, because they wouldn't give me off when my mother was very sick, I was on the verge of becoming a crew leader. Now I was ready to be given the chance to become a foreman once more. I was doing one thing right in my life anyway. My parents had taught all of their children to have good work ethics, and that was showing in my life with the promotion opportunities I had been given.

I was going out drinking almost every night, yet when Marge told me she had gone out drinking with her sister, I was jealous and distrusting. It bothered me that she had gone out drinking when she hardly ever drank otherwise. I was the one that shouldn't have been trusted, as I was out almost every night. I can remember one night when I went back to the trailer we rented right after work, and the boss thought I was sick because I didn't stop to drink on the way home. I really felt good the next day at work after a good meal and a good night of sleep, and I decided I could quit drinking. It lasted until that evening, when, being all refreshed, I stayed out until the taverns closed. I sure paid for it the next day in the hot sun. I must have drunk a couple gallons of water that day.

The owner of the company was so happy with the production we were getting that he patted me on the back and told me to take a break whenever I needed one, but to work the hell out of these guys from South Dakota. I said, "No, we work together and then break together, and that is how we are getting so much pipe placed in the ground." The first big job they had done out in the Dakotas, they averaged a leak for every half mile of pipe put in the ground. They asked me if I could knock it down to one leak every mile, and I told them we would only have one leak in the 47-mile project. When we had about 42 miles in the ground, we'd just had our first leak, and that was because a guy that hauled water shot a hole in the pipe. I couldn't blame the guy, as they were taking his job of over thirty years.

One October morning as I was driving to work, I blew out a tire on my car. As I was changing the tire, the boss of the foremen drove by me and looked at me stupidly. I finished changing my tire and reported to work seven minutes late. I could not believe it, but the head boss started yelling at me and asking where I had been. I told him that he had driven right by me as I was changing my tire. I went on to tell him that if he would've stopped to help, I would have been on time.

I'd had one previous run-in with him about a month prior to that incident: I had been putting a fire hydrant together, and

47

he got all excited because it was going too slowly. He jumped in the ditch and messed things all up. I told him to leave and come back in an hour and it would be together, which it was. He never did like me and always said I was overpaid. The problem was that if I slowed down, the whole crew slowed down. I got along great with the laborers we hired from South Dakota, and they worked their tails off for me, but didn't care for any of the other bosses.

This was like the straw that broke the camel's back. The boss told me I was acting like a child and I said, "Okay, I will." I hopped in the ditch and refused to run the caterpillar side-boom, which I had been running and not getting operator's pay to run. I was hired as a laborer and that was just what I was going to do — labor. I told my boss I had had it, and I was going to quit pipeline. He told me to just cool down and think about it. Our production was cut down to about ¼ of a normal day's production when I had been running the side-boom.

I went out that night and got smashed intentionally, and then went to work thirty minutes late so they would fire me, but they didn't. I did the same the next day, and again they didn't fire me. I was angry and there was no changing it. The boss that yelled at me didn't like it because I knew how to get the pipe in the ground and get work out of the employees. The days of high production were over as far as I was concerned. The third day that I went into work late, they finally fired me. I packed my stuff and was on my way home. I didn't know what I would do for a job, but figured I would find something. My boss gave me the names of a couple of pipeline companies that he had worked for, and he told me they could call him for a recommendation.

I packed up and headed home with mixed feelings. I didn't know what I would do for a job, but back then, jobs were quite easy to find. I drove for several hours and got home early in the afternoon. Marge didn't get excited or wonder where our next check would come from. She knew I would find a job somewhere. I did have a pretty good job performance record. I was happy to be home, but did wonder where I would find a job. It was fall and the construction companies were finishing up for the year and weren't hiring. I applied for unemployment and the company I had worked for did not contest it, so I was good for a while. I was getting enough money to live on and still be able to go out and party a few nights a week. In February of 1981, we found out that Marge was pregnant with our third child. We wanted a girl, as we already had two boys. Marge was again very proud to be carrying another baby.

Chapter 9

My New Job

I somehow made it through the winter, and then it was time to try to find a job. I was bowling in a tournament and I met the guy that had hired me to work for the state in 1972, before I had gone to work for the pipeline. He told me I had to take a test and score in the top ten percent to even get an interview, but he told me that if I was in the top ten percent, he would hire me as soon as possible. I took the test and was happy to find out I received an extra five points because I had been in the Army. I was happy to see that I was in the top ten percent without the extra 5 points, so I was sure I would get an interview.

A few days later, the guy called me and set up an interview. When I got to the interview, Les said, "Well, Jim, why do you want to work in a prison?" I told him that I had a wife and two children to support, plus one on the way, and I needed a job. He hired me on the spot, and actually put me to work two weeks earlier than I should have started, which has helped me tremendously, with seniority throughout the years for vacation picks and days off for personal holidays. I didn't know if I would like it, but I needed a job and was ready to work.

I will never forget the first day I walked into that prison. The first inmate I saw appeared to be a seven-foot-tall Indian, who scared the hell out of me just looking at him. He was probably a little shorter than that, but he looked that big. The institution I was going to be working at was a mental institution in the process of converting over to a prison. The first place they took us on our tour was to what was called

"Ward 5." This was the area that housed the most violent of the insane patients. I knew the officer working on the ward and he hollered out, "Hey, Ronnie, you have some visitors here." When I looked, I saw a man that had the biggest scarred area on his head that I have ever seen. This man used to run into steel doors headfirst. They actually had a football helmet to put on him when needed; I thought that was just something for the movies. When Ronnie approached us, my friend said, "Ronnie, give the visitors a kiss." He went right for the girl standing next to me and she grabbed my arm and almost jumped right down the stairs. I thought, "What the heck am I doing here?" I was used to bar brawling and I knew I could handle myself, but I wondered how the females were going to do against these violent criminals.

After a few days of hearing war stories about the inmates and patients, we were set out to tend to these people. The first day I worked on line, I was the charge officer on one of the patient units. Within the first hour, a patient got mad at me and began beating his radio against the wall while hanging onto the cord. I thought I was in trouble when the sergeant came up to my floor, but he told me I did the right thing by not exchanging radios with the patient. I was told every time a new officer was assigned to that unit he would try to exchange his radio, and then he would smash his when the officer didn't make an exchange.

With the patients slamming things around, yelling, and making my day miserable, the time flew by and it was time to go home. I wondered how these guards did this job day after day. After work, a bunch of us new guards went to the bar and got drunk. The next day, I went into work with a hangover and was assigned the same job again. I found out that working with the criminally insane was quite a trying job. One minute, the patient would be all right, and the next minute, they would start throwing stuff around and trying to hurt themselves.

After two days of patients, they assigned me to the segregation unit to work. The first day, I wanted to open a door and kick some punk's butt. All day long, they hollered and called us names; when they got sick of hollering, they kicked their doors. While I was training for those few days, they had a small disturbance on the segregation unit and strapped down several inmates. When you are new, you are like fresh meat to the segregation inmates. I was used to bar brawling and I had no fears of these convicts, because most of them were only bad when they had a gun.

After doing a halfway good job working in segregation, the Captain assigned me to the segregation unit every day for the next month. I didn't really care, but the noise was sickening. For a few days, we wore riot gear just to work in the block because they were throwing everything imaginable at us when we opened their trap doors to feed them. I found some of the things hilarious, just listening to these guys talk.

Finally, the captain asked me if I wanted to work the segregation unit every day. He told me, any day I wanted, all I had to do was tell him and he would remove me from that unit. I don't know what I was trying to prove, but I stayed there for five years before I switched jobs. I didn't realize what it was like to work on a unit where the inmates actually behaved somewhat. I would work overtime on the regular units, but after a while, I got so used to working segregation that it was the only job I liked.

It was October 30, 1981, that Marge told me it was time to go to the hospital to have our baby. This time I was sober for a change, and was allowed to watch as our baby girl was born. I remember trying to look to see if it was a girl or boy. Finally, the nurse said we had a healthy baby girl, who we were both very proud of.

Chapter 10

Time to Get Treatment

A few years later, I was out looking at some hunting land to lease. I was drunk again. I was so sick of being drunk, but didn't know how to stop. I looked to the west, and all I saw was a blur. That was it. I threw my can of Budweiser on the ground and asked Chuck if he would give me a ride home. He asked me what the problem was, and I told him I was sick of being drunk and I was going into treatment. All the other guys said, "Oh, come on, Zim, you are just having a bad day."

I said, "No, I've had it; I'm done with alcohol once and for all." I will never forget the look on my wife's face when I told her I was leaving. I think she thought I was leaving her, until I told her, "No, honey, I'm going into treatment to kick this alcohol addiction." She was very happy as a tear trickled down her cheek.

Time for treatment

Marge was put on this earth for a reason, I know

To straighten my behavior from years ago

I drank very heavily without a care

She knew I had a good spot, the question was where

She stayed by my side year after year

She kept on hoping sobriety was near

For years she acted as a single parent

She smiled all day to show no resent

She scolded our children with a smile,
yet they knew what she meant

Even with that gleaming smile, the message had been sent

I came home half-drunk and told her I had to leave

A tear trickling down her cheek, she didn't want to believe

Then I said, no dear, it's off to treatment I go

Her face lit up with that familiar glow

I was so grateful she had waited through those terrible years

Sobriety was coming and the end to the tears

We called the treatment center and they told me to check in the next day. I took the phone from Marge and told the lady, "I am coming in now, whether you want me or not." They decided if I was that persistent that they would take me that night. We had a friend of mine drive us to the treatment center, and he ran a stop sign and almost got us into a terrible accident. When we got to the treatment center, they thought my friend was the person checking in, not me. Once I got checked in, Marge kissed me goodbye and I was taken to my room. I insisted that I have a single room because of what had happened to me years prior, and they allowed me a single room for a while.

After I got checked into my room, I sat in the dayroom for a little while, and they came in and offered me a cold turkey sandwich, which I accepted and tried to force down. I remember it was so dry that it stuck to the inside of my mouth. I finally forced it down and went to bed. I lay there for quite a while wondering what kind of miracle they were going to perform to rid me of the need for alcohol. I finally passed out, and it seemed like a short while later that someone told me it was time to get up.

I was escorted to the chow hall and given a hefty breakfast. I didn't really know what to do, but I found all the people were real helpful and caring. I was told that I better go make my bed and the doctor and the psychiatrist would see me that morning. The doctor asked me to verify any medication that I needed and he would verify it with my family doctor. My family doctor also had a say in if I stayed at the treatment center or not. He was pretty happy to sign me in, because he had never had a patient of his go into treatment for alcohol dependency. I don't even think he knew that I drank, or more or less had a problem with alcohol.

Next, it was time to see the psychiatrist, who was worried if I was suicidal or not. I tried to convince her that I had a problem with alcohol, and I wanted to take care of the problem and go back home. I think she was convinced that I was suicidal, even though I had checked myself into alcohol treatment.

I have failed to mention the fact that Marge and some relatives and friends had an intervention for me about a year prior to me going into treatment. I had actually told Marge that I needed help and she did all she could by setting up an intervention, but once I got there, I refused to go into treatment because it was almost hunting season for deer. Quite ironic, when I did go into treatment it was right before deer hunting season. I needed sobriety more than I needed a deer.

I noticed right away that they fed us very good food and I guessed it was because some of the people in treatment had really let their bodies go to heck. They gave us so much to do it was impossible to get everything completed and keep up with my laundry, too. Once the alcohol was out of my life, I hopped out of bed right away in the morning and got my laundry finished while most of the other people were still sleeping.

Chapter 11

The Miracle

I was having a few problems dealing with the mess I was in. I was lonely for my family and wanted to go home. I knew if I went home, I would have to pay the bill because my insurance company only paid if I completed the treatment. I didn't know which way to turn, and I don't even remember going to my room and getting down on my knees and praying. I prayed, "God, please help me, I can't handle this alcohol any longer. It is ruining my life and marriage, and I want to stop the alcohol now."

At the time I got down on my knees, my room was totally dark. All of a sudden, a bright, fabulous light lit up my room and I could see a face in the light. There were no words spoken, but somehow I interpreted that the urge to drink alcohol had been lifted from my body. During this whole experience, I could feel a slight pressure on my left shoulder, like there was a hand resting on it. That was almost 21 years ago, and I have not had a single urge to drink alcohol since that evening.

I don't know what the face was that I saw, but to me it looked like George Washington, with long, whitish hair, and it was like it was part of the light. The light was extremely bright, yet it did not hurt my eyes. There were no words spoken, but I felt that the urge to drink alcohol had been lifted from my body.

As I lay in my bed, I recalled that this was the first time I had prayed since my brother had been killed. I realized I had a life to live and I was going to do it sober. I had a great night's sleep and was awake very early in the morning. I was happy. I knew I would never drink again. I walked around like a new man and appreciated everything on earth. There was nothing that could change my mood. I didn't really know what happened that previous night, but I knew it had changed my life.

I had never heard of anything like this ever happening and I decided that it would have to be my secret. I figured if I told anyone about it, they would commit me to the house for insane people. It was fifteen years later that I told Marge what had happened, and she said that it must have been really neat. I was all prepared to defend my story and swear on a Bible that it really happened, but Marge believed me right away. The only reason I did finally tell her about my experience was because I read a book that talked about a light. A lady had died, gone to Heaven, and then come back to write a book about her experience. She also hadn't told anyone about her experience because she thought people would think she was crazy. I'd bought the book when a friend of mine told me to buy it for another friend who had just had just lost his four-year-old son in an accident. I wanted to read the book before I gave it to him, so I bought two copies.

After telling Marge about my experience, I told my children one by one, and they didn't doubt my word, either. As time went on, I began telling several people about my experience; I didn't really care if they believed me or not. I knew that it had happened, and I also knew the urge for alcohol was gone and that was all that mattered.

After my experience, the time in the treatment center went very quickly and they let me out early because they said I was a changed person. I now prayed a lot, not just for my family and myself but for all the people in the treatment center, including the staff. It seemed like no time before I was ready to give my departure speech. I wanted to mention the light so badly, but I didn't want to be laughed at or doubted. After my speech and a good night's sleep, it was time to go home.

I was standing in the hallway and my four-year-old daughter came running toward me and jumped up right into my arms. It was great. I was sober and had a family to go home to. A lot of the people in the treatment center had lost jobs and family to end up where they were. I said goodbye to my friends and counselors and we were on our way home.

I wanted to tell Marge about the light, but I knew it would have to be later in life, which it ended up being. It was time to go home and get back to work. It was time to be the father and husband I was meant to be. I found out in short time that, although I was sober, it was going to take a long time to build trust with my family. I worked very hard at it and so did my family, and after a while I built up the trust again.

A couple years down the road, we had family counseling so everyone could get used to having a sober father and husband around. We worked at it and became the best family we could. We had our bad times and disappointments, but also had our fun times.

Chapter 12

My Father's Passing

After working five years in segregation, I figured it was time to promote to sergeant. I took the test and was given an interview at an institution about thirty miles from my hometown. I was promoted immediately, and accepted the job. I worked at that institution for exactly six months, and then I transferred back to Dodge Correctional Institution. I continued to go to AA meetings and stayed sober, without ever having an urge to drink.

In 1989, my father passed away and everyone thought that his death would give me an excuse to go out drinking. I never once even thought about alcohol, and I knew how proud my father was of me for quitting drinking a few years prior. It was a tough time because he was my last parent. Marge gave me all the support in the world again, and that was much appreciated.

As the years went by, we experienced all the things that parents do, having two sons and a daughter. We raced around going to sporting events and talked to teachers when our children got into trouble. At least now we had a somewhat normal family, if there is such a thing. The years slid by and we did the best we could, raising our children and having some fun for ourselves.

Chapter 13

Marge's Illness

About mid-November of 2003, Marge complained a little bit about a backache and was spending a lot of time on a heating pad. I asked her why she didn't go to the doctor and have it checked out, and she said it would be okay. She told me she thought it was just a pulled muscle or something and it would get better. She said all they would do was prescribe some pills she didn't want. Marge was so good at hiding pain, I could never tell how much she was in. Finally, Marge went to the doctor shortly before Christmas and had some fluid removed from her lung. A couple days before the New Year, I received a call from the doctor; she wanted to talk to us about the fluid they had extracted from Marge's lung. We set up an appointment for January 2, 2004.

On January 2, we rushed to the doctor to hopefully get some good news on the fluid they had removed from Marge's lung a couple weeks prior. I knew the news was not good, or they wouldn't have requested that I accompany Marge to the doctor. I tried not to let on to Marge that I knew we were about to receive bad news, but truthfully, I think we both knew what was coming.

As expected, the doctor told us Marge had cancer and it was malignant. We hugged, we cried, and we sat staring at each other. News like this is hard to deal with no matter how hard you try. Marge had a very upbeat attitude that she would beat the cancer, and I guess I was just stunned. The first part of the battle was to have a surgery to remove the rest of the fluid and put a powder in her lung to prevent the fluid from getting into the lung again.

The Unknown Cancer

The fluid in her lungs had came from a cancer

Where it started, we had no answer

The cancer was spreading like a field on fire

The way Marge was fighting you had to admire

I prayed and wondered why it had happened to her

I kept praying they would find a marvelous cure

I was proud of the way she fought while keeping her smile

The whole time knowing her life was on trial

Marge was a person who would give anyone her last dime

I would have given everything I owned to buy her more time

Now I know that God had a plan

Her time was coming to go and meet with the Man

Our doctor pulled some strings and the surgery was set for the next week. After the surgery, the doctor said everything had gone well, and hopefully the fluid would not return. I was curious as to what the next step would be, and we were told we would be seeing a cancer doctor as soon as Marge was released from the hospital. Marge's room was filled with plants and flowers from her many friends. Marge's director (her boss — she sold Mary Kay) had given her some type of exotic flowers and nurses from several floors came to see the beautiful blooms. After she was released from the hospital, we set up an appointment with the chemotherapy doctor.

Marge had a very nice young doctor who said he was going to treat the cancer very aggressively because they didn't know its origin. We were both scared when the doctor started talking about quality of life. Marge wanted to get on with her life and didn't really have time to deal with this cancer, but we knew she had to have the treatments. I guess we knew that it would be a long battle and the results were not guaranteed. Marge could not start the chemotherapy treatments until she was healed from the surgery.

I continued to work when I didn't have to take Marge for an appointment; a lot of the time, I just worked part-time. We were a close couple and grew even closer as she battled her disease. It became a family battle, and we were determined to beat it. The doctors and nurses were so nice, and you could see the disgust in their faces when they couldn't find where the cancer had originated.

I laughed each time Marge would meet a new nurse, because she would end up selling her Mary Kay Cosmetics. It was her job, and she enjoyed it to the utmost. She had just made Mary Kay sales director the previous spring, and was doing all she could keep up with her sales while battling her disease. Marge always talked about her Mary Kay family, and also our family. Sometimes I wondered which family she was talking about.

Marge started her chemotherapy at the end of February and the first treatment went quite well. She did not get really sick like the stories we had heard about chemo patients. It did slow her down and made her sleepy, however, she handled the treatment quite well. March 4, 2004, Marge received her second chemotherapy treatment. Marge's leg hurt really badly during the treatment, but when she told the nurse, the nurse slowed the flow of the liquid and the pain stopped. The next day, Marge wrote in her journal how she couldn't believe how much energy she had.

We Prayed

We hoped and prayed for a quick recovery

Deep down I knew it would take a medical discovery

The cancer word is scary, for reasons we know

Marge was fighting hard and not letting her feelings show

The origin of the cancer was still unknown

The pain of the cancer was not fully shown

Marge was given painkillers and she took very few

She was given chemotherapy and radiation, too

Because of her treatment, she lost all of her hair

*I told her she was beautiful without it,
she shouldn't even care*

At first she wore a wig, but after a while

She walked with no hair, but a big gleaming smile

By now, I had assumed most of the duties from cooking to laundry to cleaning the house. It was nothing that any other loving husband wouldn't do. I made a lot of meals where we could eat leftovers for a couple days. I made a lot of chili and things like that, which were quick to make after work. I kind of enjoyed helping my sick wife, as she had tended to me for years whenever I was sick. We started to spend more time together than we did before. Marge didn't drive anymore, so I took over the 2003 Pontiac Grand Am she had won from Mary Kay. Of course, I was driving under her direct supervision.

The next week, Marge had a lot of pain according to her journal (the family read it after she passed), but she never did complain much. She was always so happy when her friends from Madison would come up to play Dominos. We had made an appointment to take our adopted dog to the Humane Society because it was getting to be too much with his diabetes, but when the time came to take him, I could see the look on Marge's face and I told her we could keep the dog if it meant that much to her.

Over the next few days, Marge's hands began to itch so badly that she couldn't stand it. She had to soak her hands in water with baking soda in it. I felt very helpless as there was nothing I could do to help her. I wished I could take the itching and pain from her and put it in my body. One evening, we went to meet our daughter Kari for supper and had to cut it short because Marge's hands itched so much. She couldn't even start to eat her meal because of the continual itch on her skin. We had to get a doggy bag for Marge's meal and take it home with us. We only got to see Kari for a little while and then went home to deal with the itching.

I was so angry that our insurance from the state didn't cover a different type of cream to help her with the itching. I take inmates to the hospital all the time, and they get the best treatment possible; they get all the name-brand medication, but we have to co-pay and get the generic type. Who says that crime doesn't pay? I sometimes really wonder. I bought Marge the better cream out of pocket and it helped a little bit. I had a skin cream from a while ago and it helped her quite a bit. I didn't care how much the cream cost, I didn't want to see Marge suffer if I could pay to get rid of it.

Marge started taking oatmeal baths, which seemed to help some. She also put ice on the itchy areas of her skin and took Benadryl, which helped a little, but also made her sleepy. It seemed like the itching would never end. After quite a while, the doctors got the itching under control. It was so hard to watch someone I loved suffer so much. I was helpless and could only try to comfort her the best I could.

Doctors

Doctors, hospitals, and treatments galore

When we finished with one, there would always be more

We walked out of hospitals and tried to be positive

All Marge wanted was that chance to live

Each day we were on an emotional ride

Trying to be patient and take it in stride

We searched out doctors both near and far

We just wanted to know what the chances are

The cancer spread from body part to body part

I looked at the doctors — did they know where to start?

I prayed remission would come just for a while

Through it all, Marge kept her gleaming smile

Chapter 14

Treating Cancer

Marge had kept her good spirits up and went to all her treatments for chemotherapy and the bone-builder treatment also. She continued to do as much as she could around the house, and even took a trip to a Mary Kay convention in Dallas, Texas, in July. The way the doctor encouraged her to go, I had a feeling it would be her last seminar. Her friends had to wheel her around in a wheelchair, but she had fun as usual.

I kept picking up on subtle hints from the oncologist that the cancer was getting the best of Marge; however, she continued to fight as hard as she could. A lot of the days after her treatment, we would drive out to my hunting land to cut wood or work on the food plots. Marge was happy to just sit and read a book in the shade, as she was told to stay out of the sun as much as possible. We had some nice long talks on our little trips, and we just enjoyed being outside together. Marge had a little problem walking for a distance so she took a big stick and used it as a walking stick. Each time that we left, she would lean it against a tree so it would be there the next time. I felt bad one day, because she had walked all the way into the woods and then my chainsaw didn't work properly and we had to go home after a short while.

Chapter 15

Deceased Relatives Come To Visit

Marge was having terrific headaches, and as much as she didn't like to complain, she called me at work to come home and take her to the emergency room at the hospital twelve miles from our house. It was a hospital that covered patients with our type of insurance. Our family doctor had told Marge to go there as soon as possible, so I got out of work immediately and drove her to Beaver Dam.

When we got into the emergency room, they decided to do a CAT scan on her head, which showed that the cancer had spread to her brain. The radiation clinic in Madison was very quick in getting Marge an appointment to start her radiation treatments. Each day for two weeks, we drove to Madison for her treatments. I was amazed by the number of people that I saw come to that clinic for radiation treatments. I felt so bad for all the people there.

Cancer did not discriminate by age or sex in any way. I saw a girl in her teens, ladies and gentlemen from all ages and races. It was heartbreaking to watch those people come in for treatments and then go back to their normal lives day after day. One of the young ladies was a college student, and some of the patients were working jobs yet. When we were finished with treatments, the doctors hoped the radiation had worked as well on Marge's brain as it had on her back. Time would tell, but for now, we had to deal with the rest of the cancer in her body.

I have often wondered what the results of all the other people that we saw at the radiation clinic were. I prayed that some of them beat the cancer. I was amazed at all the smiles I saw at that clinic, with the people dealing with such a disease.

I took Marge over to see our family doctor, who said to take Marge to St. Mary's Hospital in Madison and check her in through the emergency room to have surgery as soon as possible. We waited and waited, and finally the emergency room doctor came in and got all upset because they had started doing bloodwork that he felt was unnecessary. It probably was, but he seemed to take it out on Marge. I had to walk out of the room to keep from doing something I would regret later.

When I walked back into the room, he was talking to Marge and saying, "What do you want from me?" Finally, I said she wants what her doctor suggested, a surgery for outside her lung where the fluid was building up again. I was extremely angry and didn't want anyone treating my wife the way this doctor was. It was a good thing that I had anger classes while in alcohol treatment years ago. How Marge could just sit there and take his abuse, I will never know. Finally, the doctor gave her another prescription for Hydrocodone syrup, which we had several bottles of already. He then discharged Marge and told us to go home.

In all my years, I had never met a doctor with such a poor bedside manner, and it took all I had to hold back from telling him what I really thought. I didn't understand how anyone could treat such a kind lady with utter disrespect. I pushed Marge out of the hospital in a wheelchair and took her home again. When I called our family doctor on Monday, she was just irate that the doctor at the emergency room didn't admit her for surgery the following week. I took Marge over to our family doctor, and after giving Marge a check-up, she again told me to take her back to the hospital for a surgery to remove the fluid from her chest in a couple days. This time she was admitted, and a surgery was scheduled for the next day.

That night, Marge was sleeping well, so I went home to take a shower and bring some more clean clothes. I talked on the cell phone with one of Marge's friends all the way home. After I got home and called all of our children to let them know about the surgery, I took a nice hot shower and got ready for bed.

That night I got down on my knees and prayed very intensely and told God I needed help, because I couldn't deal with this anymore. I finally fell asleep after a couple hours of just laying in bed wondering what our future would be. Would Marge have a miraculous recovery, or would the cancer take over?

The next morning, I got up early, took a shower, and headed right back down to Madison. As I was driving on Interstate 90/94, I felt a presence in my car. When I looked to my right, I saw an apparition of my father. I could easily make out that it was my father, but he appeared to be transparent. He didn't say anything, and as shocked as I was, I just looked back at him, and to his right side, my deceased brother Brian appeared, followed by my mother. All I could say was, "Wow." They all appeared as kind of see-through, yet they had very distinct features that made it easy to determine who each apparition was. Then, out of thin air, my grandma appeared to the right of my mother. As I looked, I said, "What the hell are you doing here?" I hadn't liked my grandma for years because of the way she had treated my mother while they were both alive.

I'd heard of deceased people appearing to loved ones in this manner before. My brother had appeared to me after he was killed, but I had written it off as the fact that I was drunk and just imagining things. Brian had come to me in this see-through type being years ago and told me he was in a better place and not to worry about him. He also told me that it was not my fault that he had gotten shot. I thought a lot about that experience, but never did mention it to anyone for fear they would think I had gone crazy. I could remember him

69

standing there and talking to me, but I could only see him from the waist up. Within a couple of weeks, I decided that I had just imagined that my brother came to me after he died, and never really thought about it for years.

After having my father, brother, and mother appear, followed by my grandmother, I didn't know what to think or say. I mentioned it to Marge and also a friend of mine at work a couple days later. They had postponed Marge's surgery. The doctor never told our family, but he went into Marge's room and told her she didn't have long to live. I was really angry that he did that while she was by herself. He could have had the family come in and tell all of us the bad news at once.

I was getting angered more every time I dealt with the doctors at that hospital. I talked to one of the several fine nurses, and she told me that if the surgeons felt they couldn't cure the patient, they were just going to die, and they had absolutely no bedside manners when they told the patients. I was at least happy that Marge had good nurses helping her as much as they could. Marge had her surgery later that night, and after the surgery, the doctor finally told me and our children that Marge only had a couple of months to live.

We had never really talked about Marge passing on because she was determined that somehow she was going to beat the cancer. Her friend in Texas was trying to get it set up that Marge would fly down to see the doctor that she had when she beat her cancer several years ago. It took quite a bit, but we were finally getting records sent to Texas for the doctor to look at.

I was no longer working, so I spent all of my time with Marge and helped her deal with her problems the best we could. Marge hated pills, so she only took them when the pain was unbearable. She had developed a cough that kept both of us up all night. She would go downstairs, but she coughed so loud and so much that I could still hear her way upstairs. Marge didn't like being a burden on anyone, so she tried to do as much as she could. I felt good being able to help her by making her meals, which at that time was mainly just soup. I tried my best to comfort her, and we talked about several things that had happened throughout our lives. I thanked her for putting up with me through all of my drinking years. Marge continued trying to sell her Mary Kay cosmetics the best she could. She had a lot of return customers, so I helped her put the orders in bags and helped make out the receipts. I can only imagine the pain she was in and she continued to smile through it all.

Chapter 16

The Last Doctor Visit

When I took Marge into the hospital to see her cancer doctor, I noticed she was much weaker than she had been. Marge still wanted to fly to Texas and have her friend's doctor check to see if he could help. Her doctor told her at this point that it would probably be more harmful than any good for her to fly with her health the way it was. Marge was concerned about her treatment to keep her bones strong and the doctor told her she would not be getting it that day. At that time, I felt the doctor was giving up hope of any type of recovery for Marge.

I had to wheel her out of the hospital in a wheelchair and it was hard to get her back into the car. As we were driving home, Marge insisted that I get out of the house and go bow hunting that evening. I had to go to the pharmacy to get her some higher-dose morphine pills, but I had to wait for her sister to come over so I could go. I would not leave her alone for even a minute. I had a very hard time getting her up the steps and into the house.

Marge said, "Maybe this is God's way of showing me how your breathing is, by not allowing me to get any air." Marge even had a smile as she said that. I have emphysema from years of smoking that didn't go away after I quit. I sure didn't think God was punishing Marge for anything. We all sin, but Marge was as close to a saint as I had ever met. Many times, I had wondered how I was so lucky to have such a beautiful and understanding wife. Marge stayed with me through years of alcoholism, just hoping maybe someday I would quit, and that day had come about nineteen years ago. As soon as her sister came, I drove to the pharmacy and picked up her new pills. She smiled and insisted that I go hunting and get out of the house for a while. As sick as she was, she still worried that I had been tied down to the house too much. She worried that she was too much of a burden on me. That is just the type of lady she was, always putting other people in front of her needs.

My son and his friend picked me up, and we went to the hunting land. I did not have hunting on my mind and just wanted to get home to Marge. As we were driving home, my phone rang just as we passed the church where we had been married over 32 years ago. I knew it wasn't good, and didn't want to answer the phone. It was Marge's sister; she asked how far we were from home. I told her about half an hour, and she said that Marge was starting to go downhill and that she had notified our other two children. I could not imagine the thought of living without Marge after all we had been through.

As we drove home, I started to think back to all the things we had been through together. Four months before our wedding, she'd held me so tightly the night my mother passed away. Six months after our wedding, my brother was shot to death in a family dispute, and she did everything she could to help me live with my grief. Then I turned more to alcohol and the disease progressively got worse. How any spouse could put up living with an alcoholic for over twelve years I will never know, but I am forever grateful that she believed in me. Then, four years into my sobriety, my father passed away. A lot of my friends thought that I would be back drinking with the loss of my father. They just didn't know that God had lifted the urge for me to ever drink again. All the way home, we were talking, but I didn't really hear a word that Brian or his friend said. I was too busy thinking of all the fond memories and the upsets we had been through.

When we pulled up to our house, I saw that there were a large number of cars parked all the way up the street. As close to the end as it was for Marge, she still managed to smile as I entered the house. I felt so selfish that I had gone hunting, even though Marge had insisted I go. Friends and relatives kept arriving, and a short while later, our daughter Kari arrived. Flo, my sister-in-law, had called our other son, Tim, and he was on his way home, also.

Marge kept asking if Tim was there yet. This was between 10:30 and 11 p.m.; at that time, Tim attempted to call home on his cell phone but his phone went haywire. The lights on his phone kept flashing and all kinds of weird signs flashed across the front of his phone. It kept flashing, and #&2tw87*zu#%8#29* appeared across the screen. Of course, that is not the exact form of the symbols, but it was on that order. As close as we could figure, Tim's phone was going haywire at the time Marge was asking about him. Tim tried everything, but could not get his phone to work. He tried turning it off and on again, but it would not work. Finally, he took out the battery and recharged the phone to call home and talked to my sister-in-law. What caused this malfunction in Tim's cellular phone we can only guess, but I'm sure Marge had something to do with it.

Chapter 17

Final Goodbye

As I held my wife's hand, I knew it would be over shortly. A beautiful life was about to end. Marge was one of the most loving and caring people around, and she was my wife. She was the true meaning of unconditional love. She would give anyone her last dime, or just a kind smile, or some encouraging words to help make their day special.

A couple days earlier, I had been exhausted from being awake so many hours. I heard Marge talking, and she wasn't talking to me. I was the only person in our living room besides her, so I just listened. I did not make out anything specific that she was saying, but as I watched, she nodded her head and replied, "Yes, uh-huh, okay." She looked as though she was receiving some special instructions from someone.

When she was finished talking, I asked, "Who were you talking to?"

Marge looked at me as though I should naturally understand and said with a very quizzical look on her face, "The angels. Who do you think I'm talking to?"

All three of our children had arrived from different parts of the state and several of her relatives and friends were also present. I had become very angry earlier when one of her friends who used to be a nurse tried to put a morphine pill in her mouth. Marge did not like drugs and used them only when the pain was unbearable. She had given birth without a block with two of our three children. She used to get her teeth drilled without even being frozen. She had a much higher tolerance for pain than I ever had. A while later she did take a morphine pill, because the pain was just too much for her. During her fight with cancer, we had accumulated several bottles of painkillers, which ended up being flushed down the toilet because she took so very few of them. The only pills she took most of the time were the ones she thought were going to make her better.

I held on to Marge's hand for most of the last few hours for her on earth. When she could no longer talk, I got up and walked a few steps away so one of her sisters could hug her. I was telling her friends and relatives that on our first date, I'd spent my whole check trying to win her stuffed animals at the fair, and when I took her home, she wouldn't even kiss me goodnight. Marge looked up and said, "Come here, hon," and she kissed me. Those were the last words I ever heard her speak on earth. I knew it was almost over and I told God it was time to take this very special person home.

I whispered very softly, "I love you, hon," and as I looked at her lips, I saw them move ever so slightly to say, "I love you, too, hon." As our family held on to her arms and hands, she passed on peacefully at 1 a.m. I was watching as she passed, and I observed what appeared to be her soul passing out of the top of her head. Her body, which had been cold and clammy, instantly became warm. I did not tell anyone about watching her soul leave her body because I didn't want people to think I had gone crazy. I had never witnessed the final moments of anyone's life, but one of her friends who is currently a nurse said that when most people pass, the room gets very cold. When Marge passed, the room was very warm.

After having the coroner and police at the house, my friend who is a mortician asked if I wanted to help put my wife in the body bag, which I did. I helped to carry her earth body out to the hearse, and then softly said goodbye to my wife of over 32 years. I said goodbye to Wayne and told him I would meet him at the funeral home at ten in the morning.

After I got back into the house and the friends and relatives were leaving, my oldest son told me I wouldn't believe what had just happened. He went on to tell me that his mother had taken him by his hand and taken him to the gates of Heaven. He said Marge showed him a big wooden door, but she wouldn't let him look past it.

Celebrating An Angel's Life
By Gail Renderman

"I have fought a good fight, I have finished my course, I have kept the faith"
II Timothy 4:7

Cry for Marge not,

But celebrate her life with happy thoughts

The warmth in her heart, the sparkle in her eyes

Her friendly "Hello" to all who came by

Her delight in fun times with family and friends

The humor in her soul, her laughter didn't end

The love for her family, her strength through the fears

The good times we've shared with her throughout the years

How she achieved MK Directorship after years of setting goals

The kind things she did for others and never said "no"

She faced each challenge with humor, courage, and grace

She could light up a room with just the smile on her face

Yes...Celebrating Marge's life is easy today

Because this Angel touched so many lives along the way

We'll remember her warmth when the sun shines bright

We'll remember her sparkling eyes in the stars at night

We'll remember her sweet spirit when we look at the flowers

We'll remember her through jokes and how we laughed for hours

It's our turn now to see her work through,

To brighten the lives of others as Marge would do

God's given her Angel Wings to watch over us today,

But remember she's never far, just an angel's breath away.

He said it was just like a picture Marge and I had in our room of Jesus standing by a big wooden door. I believed every word of it, because I had seen the bright light and had the urge to drink lifted from me during alcohol treatment. If that was possible, surely it was possible for Marge to show Brian the gate to Heaven. My oldest son, Brian, did not believe in God before this experience, but he sure does now. Although it took me about fifteen years to talk about my experience in the treatment center, Marge and I talked about things like that quite a bit in the years following.

I had always figured I would die before her, and I told her I would brush up against her in the funeral home to let her know I was all right. She always joked, "How do you know you will die first?" I told her because of the life I had lived compared to her saintly life, I had to go first. She always had her very special smile and said that I didn't know that. I said if she went first, to let me know somehow that she was all right.

The next day was one of the worst days of my life, as our immediate family had to pick out a casket for Marge. When we walked into the room, we all walked directly over to a casket with a pink interior which we picked out without even looking at the price. Marge was a Mary Kay Director, and pink was the color it had to be. Later that afternoon, I took my two sons and daughter to Madison to buy some clothes for the funeral. As we were going up an escalator, the song "Power of Love" by Celine Dion began playing loudly throughout the mall. We all almost stopped in our tracks, as that had been one of Marge's favorite songs. Marge had a very beautiful voice and sang along with it on the CD in her car. When Marge thought I was sleeping, she would really get into it, which I loved. If you ever really listen to the words of that song, they are very powerful!

Our family honored Marge's request and we had a closed casket; Marge always said she didn't want people gawking at her in the funeral home. Before we closed the casket, I gave Marge our last kiss on the lips and said goodbye *one more time*.

Standing in the front row of the over-packed church, I closed my eyes very tightly and saw a vision of Jesus Christ in a purple robe with his hands open, welcoming Marge home. I have tried closing my eyes on several occasions since to see if I could get the same vision, and I absolutely can't. It was an amazing sight to my closed eyes, which I will always remember. One of Marge's close friends asked if she could sing at the cemetery and release balloons, which was an old Irish tradition. We are not Irish; however, I told her that would be just wonderful.

When we lose a loved one, we always want that one last kiss, the one last time to say we are sorry for any wrongdoing, the one more hug, the one more laugh, the one more time to hold hands — the list goes on. People tell me that at least I had time to prepare for Marge's death. Marge had been sick for almost a year. These people don't know that there is no way to plan for the loss of a loved one. One of my friends who is divorced said, "At least you got to bury your wife." I haven't figured out yet if that is a good thing or not. Marge and I didn't believe in divorce, and we worked through some pretty tough times. She had stood by me through my alcoholism, job loss, my brother being murdered, and my mother and father passing. I had to put up with her change of life, which I wouldn't wish on anyone. I could remember days when I would compliment her and she would find something wrong with my compliment. The fact was that we worked hard and made our marriage last.

When Marge and I were dating and would drive through the town I live in, she could not believe all the people that waved at me. She always joked that I must know all of the nine thousand people who lived in Waupun. I knew Marge made a lot of friends after moving to the town where I lived, but I was totally impressed by the number of people who came to her funeral and visitation. One large section of the church was filled with her Mary Kay friends. She always told me her Mary Kay friends were like family, and I now believed her. The priest told me it was the most people he had ever seen in his church, and wished that he could get that many to come on Sunday. I did not really care for school and definitely did not like poetry — I thought it was for girls, but somehow after Marge passed, words came to my mind and I wrote a little poem for her, which we printed and put in a frame and placed at the funeral home.

To the One I Love

I knew you well, I loved you so

It's really hard letting you go

You got your wings and you can fly

I can see you high in the sky

I wake in the morning and am feeling blue

But I know the love we had will pull me through

Time will heal my broken heart

But I'm not ready for that to start

Nothing can replace the time we had

But memories keep me from being too sad

Just for now, I will say goodbye

Until I meet you in the sky

I love you — Nim

"Nim" was a nickname I'd had for several years, and still have today. I was just amazed at how the words just came to me at a time of such a tremendous loss. I received several compliments about my poem and also caused several tears to flow.

Comfort

Surrounded by friends and family, yet all alone

The only one I loved, God has called home

The hugs of friends and family help ease the pain

I know my loss is my loved one's gain

But tears now flow across my face

As I long for just one more embrace

Then comfort comes and I see Christ's face

He hugs my loved one and I feel his grace

— Anonymous

Chapter 18

Living Single

After the funeral, when everyone had gone home, it was time to start learning how to live single and do all the chores that Marge used to do, also. First on the agenda was to clean Marge's Mary Kay room; I knew it was going to take weeks, if not months. I began the slow task of burning old records and sorting out the product and other paperwork, some of which needed to be kept or given away. Many tears flowed as I began that everlasting task. There are still several things in that room that I have not changed.

A few days later, as I stood looking aimlessly at nothing in particular in my dining room, I noticed that there was still a bunch of balloons that had lost nearly all of their helium hanging by the floor. I looked at them and thought, "These mean nothing anymore." I don't know what possessed me to take them outside and let them fly, as there was no wind and not enough helium to allow them to rise up in the sky. One of the balloons was plain; one had "Get Well Soon," and another had "Never Give Up" written on it.

In the last few minutes of light in the day, there was absolutely no wind as I released them one at a time. As I was preparing to let them go one at a time, the plain balloon slipped out of my hand and slowly ascended to the sky. I couldn't believe my eyes, and allowed the balloon with "Get Well Soon" written on it go; and it pulled from my hand, it raced its way rapidly skyward. It went straight up for a while, and then drifted north until I could see it as a speck in the sky a couple blocks away. In my amazement, I wondered what the next balloon would do. I then released the final balloon with the words "Never Give Up" printed on it, and it sailed slowly over my neighbor's fence and appeared to go down. As I watched it slowly rise, it continually gained speed until it was out of sight.

With tears running down my cheeks, I looked up and said, "Thanks, Marge." I knew this was her way of showing me she was all right. This was just the beginning of spiritual things happening to me. I'd previously had visions of the dead and was surrounded by the light in treatment, but these were the first signs from Marge.

A few days later, I was standing in the living room when a small picture flew off a wooden shelf one way, while the holder went the other way. At first it didn't hit me, but then I thought it had to be Marge again. There was no draft in the house, no open doors or windows, and no fans running. I had read a couple of books that talked about spirits moving objects like that to let their loved ones know they are all right. It was fine with me, and I prayed that she would keep giving me those little signs. I miss her physical being so much, yet it helps to know that she was all right and lives on after this life on earth. There is such a comfort knowing she lives on.

God has allowed me to be comforted by Marge's spirit so that I can pass that comfort on to our children and relatives.

To the One I Love — part 2

It was one month ago today

The good Lord came and took you away

You drifted away with a slight smile on your face

Because you knew you were going to a better place

You went to a place not far from here

I know that's true because I feel you so near

While on earth, you were a person everyone adores

So God made a special place for a soul like yours

I'm sure we will meet again in the light

I long for that day so I can hold you so tight

For now, I will live without the physical you

Until I ascend to Heaven, where the skies are so blue

I love you — Nim

On November 13, 2004, which would have been Marge's 53rd birthday, a benefit was held for her to help pay the outstanding medical bills. This benefit had been planned for October, but we cancelled due to Marge's passing. At the benefit, I was talking to one of Marge's brother's wives and she told me I wouldn't believe what had happened. She went on to tell me that she had been standing in her bedroom looking into her big mirror, when she saw Marge standing there. I told her, "Yes, I believe it 100%," and told her of some of my happenings.

I then talked to another of Marge's close friends, and she told me how she had hoped and asked for a signal from Marge showing she was all right. Gail said that as she was standing by a picture that had been hanging on a wall for a long time, it fell down. Gail smiled and placed it back on the wall, only for it to fall off again. This continued for several days, until Gail finally left the picture sitting on the desk. Gail then stated Marge must have gotten mad, and down came the new false ceiling that was being installed. Gail had been a very special friend of Marge's for several years. Gail had given Marge the helium balloons that flew high into the sky with no helium in them.

December 1, 2004

<u>To the One I Love — Part 3</u>

I asked for a sign from up above

You gave me several to show your love

You knocked the picture off the shelf and onto the floor

Just to let me know you were okay; still,
I yearned for you more

You took the balloons from my hand and let them fly

Until all I could see was a speck in the sky

Our love didn't end, it's just been put on hold

It will resume again in Heaven, so I am told

I want to hold you and have just one more kiss

Your lips brushing lightly against mine so dearly I miss

All time stopped for me on that fateful night

Yet I knew you were okay, you were heading for the light

I love you — Nim

With the holiday season fast approaching, my daughter Kari convinced me to let her put up a small Christmas tree and a few decorations. This was Marge's favorite time of the year, and she would put decorations all over the house until I hardly had room to lay my hat.

I walked into the house about a week before Christmas, and a little puppy with a pink ribbon around her neck came walking up to me. My children had driven from central Wisconsin to southern Illinois to pick up this little pug for me! I had mixed feelings at first, but knew I would keep her. I named her "Ellie," and she has been a great companion for me ever since.

"I love you all dearly
Now don't shed a tear
I'm spending my Christmas
With Jesus this year
Merry Christmas from Heaven"

I didn't have much of an urge to go Christmas shopping; however, I did manage to get out and buy a few gifts.

Merry Christmas, Hon

Three months have passed since God took you away
I think about you night and day
Some days I sit at home and cry
God took you home and I don't know why
The holidays are empty without you, hon
Life seems meaningless and just no fun
I miss your smile, your gentle touch
I miss it all so very much
I sit at work with tears in my eyes
I sit and wonder, "Why, oh why?"
The stores were filled with holiday cheer
My heart was empty because you were not here
Life goes on day after day
I know I will make it somehow, some way
I love you — Nim

After things settled down a little bit and I got past the holidays, I moved back upstairs to our bedroom. The temperature in our room had always been cold in the winter. I was warm enough, but Marge always put on flannel pajamas and cuddled up to me to stay warm. It was pretty cold outside, but I kept kicking my covers off at night because it was so hot in my room. I never touched any of the settings in the basement, because the damper was already wide open. In the summer, the central air never cooled off our room enough either, so we always had to put a small air conditioner in our window. I don't have to do that anymore, and I actually get too cold at night in the summer and too warm in the winter. The only way I can explain it is, "Thank you, Marge!"

January 1, 2005

To the One I Love — part 4

Another month has gone by, day by day

I prayed to God and asked him why I had to stay

He told me I had a job on earth to do

I couldn't come join you until my mission was through

What mission I was given, I do not know

I'll know it's over when it's time to go

I live each day the best I can

Because someday I will have to answer to the Man

I love you — Nim

Chapter 19

17 Kisses

As I sat at work one day in February feeling very lonely, I thought of how nice it would be to have just one more kiss from Marge. I then felt the lightest kissing on my lips, which continued for several times. As tears ran down my cheeks, I ran into the side room and said, "Hon, that must have been 20 times."

I heard Marge say, "No, 17."

I stood in the side room for a long time before I regained my composure and went back to my desk. I work in a prison, so it was a good thing all the inmates were locked in at that time. When I sat back down at my desk and looked at my digital clock, it was 10:17. I thought, "What is up with the number 17?" This was the beginning of the number 17 becoming significant in my life. I don't know what significance it has, but it keeps popping up all over the place.

To the One I Love — part 5

I see our children as much as I can

I long for their faces to smile again

They have had a tough time, just like their dad

It's hard to smile when you're feeling so sad

We know we will all unite again

It will be in Heaven, the question is when

Just like their father, they long for one more embrace

Just one more time would bring that smile to their face

Like their father, they're waiting on time

When their times come, they'll make the Heavenly climb

I love you — Nim

March 18, 2005

This was just another normal day, and I got up and went to work early, like I normally do. The inmates were on good behavior, and it was an uneventful day. I don't know if they know when something is wrong or if they had heard us talk about my loss on one occasion. At any rate, for the past few months, it hadn't taken much to set me off, and I displayed none of the tolerance at work that I normally would have. It is hard to remain professional on nonprofessional pay, with all the daily negativity around you.

I couldn't help but have thoughts like, "How could God take my loving, caring wife at 52 years old, but allow all these criminals to live?" My wife had never done anyone any wrong in all her life, and these people had raped, robbed, killed, molested, or done numerous heinous crimes to society.

One of my friends said to me that day, "You sure are handling your loss quite well." Little did she know that every morning before work and every evening after work, I cried until I had no more tears left to shed. That day was no different, and after work, I had several periods of just crying. I did manage to hang a couple sheets of drywall in a closet I had been working on. After supper and doing a couple of loads of laundry, I went to bed early to read a book. I anticipated there might be overtime the next day, and I wanted a good night of sleep so I could work a double shift if offered the opportunity.

After letting Ellie out to do her nightly duties, we headed up to bed. Because of the pain medication I take for my back, I was falling asleep while reading my book. After putting my book on the shelf, I just stared at the ceiling for a while. All of a sudden, Ellie started looking at the door to the storeroom and growled very softly for a long period of time. After I told her to be quiet and petted her for a while, she fell asleep.

All of a sudden, my waterbed was rolling as if someone had just jumped on it. I looked at Ellie, but she was snoring and motionless. I thought I must have moved and made an air bubble move the water, but it didn't stop. All of a sudden, I could hear Marge's very distinct giggle. Marge's giggle was known to friends, like Julia Roberts' scream is known to her admirers. After a couple minutes, I just smiled and said, "Goodnight, hon."

A couple months later, I was reading one of the spiritual books I had bought, which explained how animals have the perception to see spirits that humans can't. I have found that on several occasions that Ellie growled softly, Marge would visit later in the night.

March 22, 2005

After a normal day of work, cleaning house, making supper, doing dishes, and going grocery shopping, I went to bed with a book in my hand. As usual, I fell asleep reading and I woke up to shut the lights off and go back to sleep a couple hours later.

I then had the most terrible dream of my life: it was a total replay of the night Marge passed over. I saw her, her hair about ½" long from the chemotherapy; she was sitting in the hoist chair that we had borrowed from a friend. She asked if Tim was there yet. Tim had to drive from La Crosse, about 2½ hours away. Marge did pass on a short while after Tim arrived.

The house was filled with family and friends, just like when Marge passed, and it was just like a replay of her death. At the time, I could not figure any significance of the dream; I thought maybe I missed something the night she passed, but I did not pick up on anything new in the dream.

March 24, 2005

I was so very lonely that day, and the day dragged on like it would never end. I worked first shift on overtime and wanted to work second shift also just to pass the time, but I was not offered a job. While I'm at work, I can keep my mind off my loss somewhat, and also have time to think about the spiritual things that have happened to me. It had been one of those days that I just wanted to go to bed and wake up to another day, hoping it would be better.

I went to bed early, and once again, Ellie was letting out a soft growl and looking at nothing in particular that I could see. I remembered what had happened the last time Ellie had acted that way, and I wanted it to happen again. I tossed and turned for a couple hours, trying to fall to sleep, anticipating something happening from Marge. Ellie continued to growl very softly, once in a while moving her head as if watching something. I continued to stare in the direction she was looking, but I saw nothing special or out of the ordinary. I finally drifted off to sleep to have the most wonderful experience happen.

I don't know when it happened, but all of a sudden, I felt myself heading toward Marge at an enormous speed. This, in my mind, was impossible, yet it was happening. Marge was floating in midair, a very loving smile gleaming on her face. Marge's hair was about shoulder length, and she had on a beautiful white-feathered outfit. She had the exact same smile on her face that she'd had in one of our wedding pictures. She looked the age she had been when I first met her. She looked like she had in what I considered to be the prime of her life, in all the time I knew her.

As I zoomed toward her, the smile on her face grew bigger and bigger. When I reached her, it was as though we made love. Not as we would have on earth, but like we kind of melted together; the immense feeling of love was much greater than I'd ever had on earth or could even try to explain. It was a feeling of total satisfaction, pleasure and unconditional love, all at once.

My journey didn't last long, and I woke up with my pillowcase saturated with tears. I continued to cry for a little while, until I remembered what had just happened to me. For the rest of the night, I just lay there thinking about my experience. Although short-lived, it had been a beautiful and unexplainable journey. A couple of days later, while reading a book about afterlife encounters, I realized I had experienced an out-of-body experience.

Although I had very little sleep, my next day at work was enjoyable; I walked around with a smile on my face all day. I was once again convinced that Marge was all right, and I could tell the cancer was gone by her good looks. I was in a state of euphoria, as I now began to realize the significance of the previous dream of watching her pass again: I feel that she had been showing me when she was sick and hurting and that now she was cancer-free and beautiful on the other side.

March 29, 2006

I continued to read spiritual books, and always found something interesting in the books I read. It is a year after my first out-of-body experience, and I just read in a book about what the experience I had is called: what I had explained as "melting together," the author called *merging*. It is defined as two souls literally blending together, physically, spiritually, and emotionally into a state of mutual bliss. I always love reading things that corroborate my experiences.

For quite some time, I was unsure of myself. I was deeply grieving, and thought anything could be possible with my imagination.

I have read several books that talked about what our loved ones look like on the other side. One book said that if you passed away at 60 years old, you would look 60 years old. A different book said that you could be whatever age you looked and felt the best at. Another book said that when you first cross over, you look like you did when you died and after a short period of time, you appear as you did at the prime of your life. When I saw Marge the second time, she appeared to be the age she had been when we started dating. I have a photo where she is wearing the same outfit as she had in my out-of-body experience; that photo was taken when she was in her early 40s.

I have also read that when you have visions of passed loved ones, they might be wearing their favorite dress or shirt, or perhaps you can even smell the cologne that they wore while on earth. However, I did know this was more than just a vision because I have had those before. Marge appeared as she looked on earth years ago.

I had typed my experience on my journal and wrote it like this:

> *Marge, it was so special last night being with you. It was like the first time, and then I woke up and realized it was just a dream — or was it?*

I printed this out and showed it to one of my female co-workers and told her about my experience. It is much easier to talk to females about things like this; I had mentioned one incident to one of my male friends, and he looked at me like I was crazy. Two days later, I was reading a nonfiction book about a young girl who would quite often take trips to Heaven with her deceased older brother. I was convinced that I had experienced an out-of-body experience, and I hoped that there were more to come. I ran up the stairs to show Rosanna and tell her that this was what I'd had, an out-of-body experience.

To the One I Love — part 6

I woke up this morning with a smile on my face

Last night, Marge took me to a wonderful place

We made love like we never did before

Unlike on earth, but so very much more

I had taken a trip, just me and my soul

Getting to Marge in the distance was my only goal

We melted together in a showing of love

We did it all from so high up above

I reached Marge in Heaven just for a while

I woke in the morning with a great big smile

I walked all day with my head held high

For I had found my loved one in the sky

Chapter 20

Words from Marge

My daughter planned a trip to Colorado to visit a friend, and I planned to take a trip to Las Vegas with two young ladies from work as soon as my daughter got back from Colorado. We planned it this way so that we could take turns dog-sitting. Kari was flying into Milwaukee from Denver on Easter evening.

I had a hard time going to visit my in-laws, because just being around all her family would make me very lonely. To my surprise, I stayed a lot later than I had planned and I had to rush to get to the airport in time. I don't normally speed, but when I looked down at the speedometer, it was registering 85 miles per hour. I wasn't really going any faster than the rest of the traffic, though, so I continued to speed.

All of a sudden, I heard a voice say, "Slow down, the plane is going to be late; it is going to land at 9:17." The voice in my head was that of my deceased wife, Marge. I couldn't believe what I was hearing, but I slowed down anyway. The airplane was supposed to land at 9:04 — right as I walked up to the arrival board, which said flight 4610 from Denver was expected late and would land at 9:24. A short time later, I looked at the board again; it said flight 4610 had landed at 9:17. I was almost in shock, and couldn't wait to tell my daughter; I felt I could tell her and my two sons, but nobody else, because I felt they would think I was nuts and send me to the funny farm.

The next morning, I woke up wondering how Marge could have known that a plane would land at a certain time, and also how she could talk to me. I have since read several books by some very prestigious authors and authorities on death, souls, out-of-body experiences, and near-death experiences, and I find all my experiences easy to deal with.

Amy, Lisa, and I had roundtrip tickets for Las Vegas that afternoon, and we were all ready for the trip. While having a soda and talking at the airport bar, we missed the boarding call and almost the flight, but luckily we made the flight and were off to Las Vegas. Lisa and Amy didn't gamble and I didn't drink, so we made a fine group. On our flight, I told the two young ladies about how Marge had told me about Kari's flight and the time it would be landing, as well as the other 17s that were popping up in my life.

We landed quite late at night, and by the time we got situated at the hotel, it was around midnight. I went to bed at around 4 a.m. and was showered and playing blackjack at 6:50 a.m. A while later, I noticed a young lady, about 21 years old, looking at all the tables in the blackjack area as though she was looking for someone, and then sat down right next to me even though there were several open chairs at the table where I was playing.

We immediately began talking as though we were long-lost friends who hadn't seen each other for a long time. It was unbelievable how much she resembled Marge when she had been around 21. She also had the same demeanor as Marge, and her goofy little giggle that I already missed so much. We played cards and talked for about five hours. I felt comfortable, like I had known her forever, and free to talk to her about anything. I told her about the voice telling me about my daughter's plane landing at 9:17, and we discussed my wife and her passing over in detail.

She told me that numbers were signs from our loved ones in which they were trying to tell us something. As she got up to walk away, she told me I would get plenty more signs and to write about them. As she slowly walked away, I realized I had not even gotten her name. She then looked back at me, smiled, and disappeared as if into thin air. I didn't tell my friends; however, everywhere we went, I was looking for the beautiful young lady. I never did see her again on our trip, but have very fond memories of her and think of her quite often.

I couldn't believe it, but our mini-vacation was over and it was time to fly back to Wisconsin. I didn't even notice it, but the airline switched our seats from row 15 to row 17. Lisa and Amy did, and they laughed about it later. We flew to Denver, where we had several problems finding a safe plane to fly us to Madison, Wisconsin. At one point, we were just ready to take off when the very distinct smell of burning oil caused us to switch to yet another airplane. When we finally landed, the flight attendant announced that we had landed in Madison, where it was slightly cloudy, and the time was 11:17. Both Amy and Lisa looked at me with a startled look on their faces, and we just smiled at one another.

To the One I Love — part 7

Each day arrives with a new blessing

The strength we get from faith keeps us from guessing

We don't have to wonder about the afterlife

I know it will be great, I'm told by my wife

Her words of encouragement just keep me on going

The hurt that I carry, I try to keep from showing

Someday, I will join her in Heaven above

Again, I will show her all of my love

I love you — Nim

Chapter 21

A Trip with Marge

After being back at work for a few weeks, I finally had a workman's compensation hearing scheduled for April 5, 2005, for a lung injury I had gotten at work. I told one of the captains at work that I needed a few hours off on the morning of the 5th, and he told me he would take care of it.

In 24 years working for the state, I never once missed a phone call in the morning. Having three children, you become accustomed to getting phone calls late at night for various reasons. When Marge was alive, I would usually let her answer calls to see if they were my employer trying to order me to come in early to work. Marge hated telling white lies that I wasn't home. On one occasion, the supervisor kept telling her, "Marge, this is Dodge Correctional calling. Are you sure Jim is there?" She said I was, and they ordered me into work two hours early when I already had to work a sixteen-hour shift. She giggled and smiled as she kissed me goodbye that morning.

The night of April 4th, I was sleeping normally and I remember going someplace with Marge. I don't remember any details, but I remember being with Marge and her telling me I had to get back, because my telephone was ringing. I remember rushing back from wherever and feeling a *clunk* into my body, and then getting up to answer my telephone. On days that I work, I officially start at 6 a.m., but if I'm not there by 5:40 a.m., the people at work think there is something wrong. I usually walk into work by 5:30 a.m., and my friends are used to that.

I picked up the phone and Amy asked, "Where have you been, are you coming to work?"

I said, "No, I have a workman's compensation phone conference and I will be in later."

Amy asked, "Why didn't you answer your phone when Floyd called you five minutes ago?"

I replied, "That's because I wasn't here!" Of course, supervisors never make mistakes, but mine forgot to take me off the work schedule. I ran down the stairs and listened to my answering machine; sure enough, Floyd had left me a message five minutes earlier.

After reading numerous books about near-death experiences, out-of-body experiences, and life after death, I have gained a little knowledge about out-of-body experiences. Some studies have been done that claim that more than a third of the people in the world have out-of-body experiences, but don't normally remember very much of the journey. The parts of my journeys that I do remember are that I was with Marge, and that is what gives me so much joy and hope, and allows me to look forward to meeting her again when I cross over. I have read in spiritual books that our souls are connected to our human bodies by a cord, and if the cord is severed, you are dead.

April 13, 2005

After I came home from work, I found an astonishing thing happening in my kitchen. Marge had a little four-colored plastic bird hanging by the kitchen window; the colors were light purple, green, white, and yellow, each separated by a thin strand of silver wire. I looked at the north wall and saw several reflections of the bird on the wall. That, by itself, wouldn't be all that interesting, except for the fact they were all dancing on the wall. I was amazed, because the bird was hanging perfectly still; there were no windows open, no clouds in the sky, and nothing in particular to make them dance. I watched in astonishment, noticing that there were seventeen reflections dancing on the wall. This continued until I walked away in amazement. Two days later, after work, I had the same exact scenario with the seventeen reflections of the colored bird dancing on the wall. That bird has been hanging in the same place ever since, but I have never seen the dancing reflections again.

A couple days later, I was driving to Beaver Dam to buy some groceries and a few other items. On my way there, I had to drive directly past the cemetery where Marge is buried, so I figured I would stop on the way. I signaled and progressed into the left lane to make a left turn. I saw a car full of teenagers go speeding by on my right. I was nearly parallel with my wife's grave, so I glanced over that way and heard her say, "Look out!" As I looked forward, the young driver had cut in front of me. I quickly hit the brakes and steered toward the shoulder. Luckily, I missed hitting their car by inches. They just kept right on going; I don't think they even realized that they had almost run me off the road. Good thing I had a co-pilot, or we could have all been seriously hurt or even killed. I don't know if it was Marge, my guardian angel, or what, but I'm sure happy that it was with me on that day.

As much as I hate to assume the duties of housecleaner, I realize it has to be done. Dusting is definitely one of my least favorite jobs. After going to the store and picking up some extra cleaning supplies, I thought it was time to give the kitchen a good cleaning. I cleaned the cupboards and put a lot of things I would not be using in plastic totes for the children to sort through. After all, how many things does a single man need in his kitchen? To be honest, I didn't even know what some of the things were used for.

Actually, I had done a lot of cooking before, when Marge and I were both working, and even more when Marge became sick. I did the basics: hot dishes, roasts, chicken, steak, and chili. When I was finished with the cupboards, I cleaned around the microwave and the breadbox, which Brian had built in school. It was amazing how many years we had that breadbox. I moved all the things around and scrubbed the countertop thoroughly, and then I cleaned the refrigerator and the oven.

A couple days later, standing in my living room, I heard a *clunk* from the kitchen area. The noise I heard directed me to the microwave, and the breadbox area. I looked and saw a little ceramic holder, shaped like a club in a deck of cards, lying on the counter with its top off. When I approached, I saw that there were two rings on the counter, which had evidently been in the holder. One of them was a "mother's ring" that I had given Marge several years ago, with the birthstones of each month in which our children were born.

Once again, a force had come from somewhere to knock this container from where it had been sitting. Once again, there had been no wind or other force that could have moved the container. The cat was in the room with me, and the pug can't jump that high. From what I have gained from several spiritual books, the authors say it takes quite a force to move heavier objects. This little ceramic holder weighed quite a bit for its size, but I did not see it when I cleaned the kitchen, so I don't know where it originally was sitting. I knew Kari would be very happy to have that ring, and I couldn't wait to give it to her. As strong-willed as she is, I still saw a glimmer of a tear in Kari's eye when I gave it to her.

Chapter 22

Prayer

I believe in God, especially after I was overwhelmed by the beautiful bright light while I was in treatment. I try to pray every night, but it is usually while I am in bed after reading. I had heard on several occasions about people being visited by deceased loved ones, but never believed it until I was visited by my father, brother, mother, and grandmother. I say them in that order because that is the order they came into my view. Many things had already happened that I knew were coming from Marge's soul, yet I always checked and want that *one more time!*

The few times that I have gotten down on my knees and really asked for something meaningful, my prayers have been answered — such as the incident with the light while in alcohol treatment, and when I asked for help while Marge was very sick in the hospital. I told God I couldn't handle it by myself, and the next day four relatives came to me in a vision. This in itself showed me there is an afterlife, and that Marge would be all right and cancer-free.

Once again, on a lonely evening, I got down on my knees and prayed very intensely to God, asking him to allow Marge to give me just one more signal that she was doing fine. A couple of times while conversing with Marge, I'd asked her to knock over the little figurine on our television if she was so strong. Each time I would hear a voice in my head stating, "I don't want to: I will break it."

I then would say, "Well, then, tip over the little angel on the end table." When I got home from work the next day, both the figurines were lying down, the angel on the end table and the mother-and-baby figurine on the television stand. It is possible that either the cat or dog could have knocked them over, but very unlikely: there are too many other objects very close to each of them that would have also been knocked over.

That night, I went to bed thinking about all the different things that had happened, and how lucky I was to have all those signs. I remember turning off the television in my bedroom and placing the remote up on the shelf above my bed, so Ellie couldn't step on it and turn the television on in the middle of the night. After sleeping quite soundly — which doesn't happen very often with my arthritic back — I awoke to the television playing very loudly. As I shut it off, I looked at my digital clock to see how much more time I could sleep before I had to get up for work. I saw that it was 2:17 a.m. — imagine that!

On several occasions, I have gotten up in the morning to find lights on that I knew I'd turned off the night before. I am trying to teach her to go around and turn off the lights I leave on unintentionally. She used to follow me around the house and turn off lights after me. We probably saved hundreds of dollars throughout the years by Marge turning off lights that I left on. Marge came from a large family, and I'm sure they were coached to turn off lights when not needed. I probably was, too, but never paid much attention.

Chapter 23

Voices

Since the time I was kissed lightly on my lips 17 times and was told my daughter's airplane would land at 9:17, I have listened and heard Marge talking in my head almost daily. I don't know if it took time for us to realize that we could communicate this way, or if it just happened after a while. Most of the times when I hear Marge, she is a voice in my head, which I learned is called "clairsentience." Sometimes I will ask her advice, and sometimes she will just start talking to me. It happens especially when I am having a very down day.

At first, I thought it was just wishful thinking, but how could I account for the airplane landing at the exact time that I heard in my head? There were other examples that proved these were not mere coincidences. I was convinced after the first couple times because Marge calls me by a nickname that nobody else uses; some people call me "Nim," an old nickname, but Marge will call me "Nimmy," like she did while we were married. I can on occasion hear her goofy giggle. As I was typing this, I just heard her tell me that her giggle is not goofy.

On one occasion, I did hear her whisper to me in her actual voice. She told me to look back, and I turned so quickly that I thought my head was going to spin in a circle. I was backing out of my driveway, and when I looked back, a car was approaching that I hadn't seen when I'd initially checked. It was truly shocking to me, but after all the other things I've had happen to me so far, I just smiled and said, "Thank you."

Life goes on day after day for me, and even though I have had all these encounters, I still long for Marge's physical body. I long for that one more kiss, one more hug, one more embrace — just one more time! I now realize fully what people go through when they lose a loved one. I have lost a mother, a brother, and a father, and losing a spouse is definitely the worst. I try to keep busy, and that helps a little. I don't know how I could cope if I didn't have all these things happening almost daily. I am in a lot of pain from my arthritic back, and I'm sure that the added stress doesn't help. I really don't know how people who don't get all the signs that I do to let me know that Marge is all right on the other side cope. These are my thoughts as I wait for the next sign from Marge.

May 4, 2005

After I finished work for the day, I figured I would take a drive over to our hunting land because it was such a nice, sunny afternoon. My oldest son and I purchased the land a couple of years earlier, and Marge and I had spent a lot of time at our land in the spring and early summer of 2004. Marge loved to sit at the side of the field and read her book while I worked up the land with my four-wheeler and small plow. Marge waited patiently for the wild berries to be ready, wanting to pick them before the birds did. When we finally got a partial bucket, I accidentally dumped them all over the kitchen floor, and I never thought that we could have washed them.

I was remembering all the good times that Marge and I had at our hunting land when I approached a crossroad about two miles from her parents' home, where I saw a car lying upside down on the side of the road, with a smashed-up van close to it. Just as I began to think, "I wonder if anyone was killed in this crash," I could hear Marge say in my head that the girl had been killed. I didn't stop because all the people were gone, and the wrecker was ready to haul the vehicles away. I couldn't help but wonder if the voice in my head was correct.

The next morning at work, I asked one of my coworkers Rosie if she had heard anything about a vehicle accident by highways O and S, because she lived in that vicinity. She told me no, and I told her what the voice in my head from my wife had said, that the girl in the car had been killed. A while later, Rosie came running down the stairs and told me a girlfriend of her daughter's had been killed in that accident. We looked up at the clock, and it was 8:17 a.m. I had told Rosie what the voice in my head said prior to her or me knowing that the girl was killed, which again leads me to believe that the voice in my head was actually from Marge. Up to that point, there had just been too many voices with correct predictions for all the happenings to be coincidence.

May 7, 2005

It was a slightly rainy and cool evening, so I decided to go to the casino and play blackjack for a while. I met some people I hadn't known before that evening, and after talking about working in a prison, which people always want to hear about, I decided to take my losses and go home for the night. It was around midnight, but I had off the next day, so after the hour drive home I could sleep in the next morning.

I wished I had filled my gas tank up prior to going into the casino because it was still raining and quite cold out for not having a jacket or sweatshirt along. I quickly hopped out of the car and ran my credit card through the pump so I wouldn't have to go inside to pay for gas. After fueling up, I grabbed the door handle, to find it was locked. I thought, "Oh no, I locked my keys in the car, along with my cellular phone; it's midnight, and I am an hour away from home!" I quickly ran to the other side of the car to find that door locked, also. I was freezing and didn't have a clue what to do. I was quite sure my son wouldn't answer his telephone at that time of the night, and my other children lived too far away. I really didn't want to call a friend and try to explain to them how to get into my house, find a spare key, and drive way out to Wisconsin Dells to bring me a key. As I was standing next to the car contemplating what to do, I heard a noise, and sure enough, my lock had unlocked itself. I didn't know how that happened, but I sure was glad it had.

On the drive home, I figured out that I must have brushed against the door lock as I had exited the car to get gas. It was a warm, very grateful drive home. How the electric lock opened, I can only thank Marge. I have read in several different books how spirits like to play with electronics, such as televisions, radios, and lights, but never opening electric locks. I am much more careful now when I exit the car, and I always take my keys out, even just to fill up with gas. I don't know what the explanation was, but I sure was happy it worked out the way it did. I sure wouldn't lock my keys on purpose just to see if the lock would open again. This was just another one of those stories I didn't tell to just anyone for fear they would think I was nuts.

May 8 – 12, 2005

These whole six days were filled with more signs from Marge as our wedding anniversary approached. Several times, the phone would ring once, but nobody would be there when I picked up the telephone. Numerous times when I turned on the radio, our favorite song, "Unchained Melody" by the Righteous Brothers, would be playing. It was a song that I had wanted to play at Marge's funeral, but my oldest son did not want me to. He said, "Dad, that is your song, and we'll save it for when you die." He didn't know that several times, I had called my wife on my cell phone and played "Unchained Melody" to her from my tape player. I knew that our anniversary day was going to be bad for me and things just kept happening. So many songs kept playing on the radio from when we were first going together and first got married.

I tried to stay occupied as much as I could to keep my mind off our upcoming anniversary. As I was planting pine trees on our hunting land, Marge talked in my head continuously to let me know she was by me. I know that Marge enjoyed going to our hunting land even when she was sick because it was so relaxing for her. One of the days I was walking onto our land to plant some trees, I heard Marge say in my head, "There's my stick." I saw her walking stick that she had always propped against a tree so she could find it; it helped her to walk up the little hills and keep her balance. I took her stick home that day, and it is leaning against my house by our bushes.

I could sense Marge around me all the time that week. I knew I couldn't handle being at work, so I took off May 12th and 13th and decided to drive to northern Wisconsin to stay overnight by Marge's sister and brother-in-law.

To the One I Love — Anniversary

She pulled back her veil and I gave her a kiss

The beginning had started for the life I now miss

We joined our hands and headed down life's trail

We had tough times, but we refused to fail

We held on tight and started life's ride

My alcoholism jumped in and we started to slide

I was going nowhere, and going quite fast

At the rate I was going, our marriage couldn't last

Finally one evening, I was surrounded by light

The urge for alcohol was lifted that night

We lived our lives as we vowed we would

We tried our best, we did what we could

Then years down the road and late at night

Marge was taken by God, as she raced to the light

I love you — Nim

When I took off, I decided to get a cup of coffee at the gas station before I left for the north woods. As I parked my car behind another car, the 17 in its license plate jumped right out at me. This was the beginning of a trip full of 17s. I drove up the road a while, and just happened to look at the mile marker, which was 117. I had not looked at any other mile marker at all. I was having a very rough time, and was crying a lot. Through my tears I saw a line of cars slamming on the brakes in front of me, and I quickly hit my brakes, too. I stopped about ten feet behind the car in front of me. When I looked up I saw a sign, North 17. I looked at the car in front of me, and again, a 17 in their license plate jumped right out at me. I then looked at the digital clock in my dash, and it was 2:17. The next time I looked at a mile marker, it was marker 217. I felt as though I was being bombarded by 17s.

When I finally pulled into the driveway at my brother and sister-in-law's, I looked at my clock: it was 4:17. A couple days away was just what I needed at that time. I had a nice long talk with my brother and sister-in-law, telling them about all the contact I was having with my wife. The few days flew by, and soon I was again on the road, driving home.

As soon as I hit the road, the 17s started up again. A car turned in front of me, and the 17 on her license plate jumped right out at me. Driving down the road, I looked up to see a sign: *Wausau — 17 miles*. I am sure that sign had been there for a long time, but I had never noticed it before. Up the road a ways, there was another sign: *17 miles to Princeton*. That sign had probably also been there quite a while, but I never noticed it before. After I got home, I drove about one mile out to my son's house, and between my house and his, I saw six license plates that had a 17 in them. One of the cars ran a stop sign, and when I looked at the car, the first thing I saw was the first two numbers of the license plate — 17! I don't really stare at license plates, but the numbers just kind of jumped out at me.

To My Special Friend

Life is so different without a soul mate
My loved one has left me and gone through the gate
The gates of Heaven opened for my special friend
For her it was a new beginning, not just the end
Her mission on earth was finished, and it was time to leave
She fast-tracked to Heaven on that October eve
When she reached Heaven, she did it with a smile
She was greeted by loved ones she hadn't seen in a while
Her sickness is finished, and she suffers no more
She's got her angel wings and is ready to soar
Now she works daily, doing things angels do
She's waiting to greet us when our time on earth is through
I love you — Nim

June was a new month, and some friends, relatives, and I planned a fishing trip to Canada; I had never been there and figured getting away would do me some good. We fished for a couple of days in northern Wisconsin and then headed to Canada. It just amazed me how my wife could travel right with us. I didn't have a lot of signs from her, but once in a while I would hear her talking in my head.

We had pretty bad weather, with rain everyday and some heavy winds. We rented a houseboat, and each night we pulled it in to what we thought would be the calmest bay, but each morning we woke up to find the wind howling in our direction. One morning, we had to bail our fishing boat for about an hour until the bilge finally caught up. We still had a great time and caught plenty of fish. It was nice getting to have walleye once, and sometimes twice, a day. We couldn't bring many fish back with us, but we could eat all we wanted while we were there.

On the third night in Canada, I had my next out-of-body experience. I was sleeping quite soundly, when all of a sudden I was with Marge; we were flying and looking at all the lakes and beautiful scenery. I don't know where I was exactly, but I remember something like a *clunk* again as I re-entered my body. I didn't say anything to my friends about my special trip for fear they would rush me to the psychiatrist. I don't know how much I remember when I have these experiences, but they seem to end very quickly. Each time I have had one, I wake up very happy. The day after an out-of-body experience has always been a good day for me. I don't know if I just have a different attitude or what, but I believe the hope it gives is unequivocal. There is nothing in this world that I could compare the few seconds of memory with. The colors I have seen are different and much more beautiful than any I have ever seen on earth. The temperature seemed perfect — not hot or cold, just comfortable. I remember that the white in Marge's dress when I went to her was whiter than any I had ever seen.

Of the many books I have read that talk about out-of-body experiences, all have stated that the person experiencing does not have much of a memory after the experience. As hard as I try, I can only remember a short period of time outside of my body. When I had my first one, it seemed like it was over in seconds. I raced toward Marge, we melted together, and I woke up with a wet pillow and tears in my eyes. When I had my second out-of-body experience, it must have lasted for minutes, because the telephone calls I received were five minutes apart, and I remember Marge telling me we had to get back because the phone was ringing.

I am very happy that I have had these experiences, and I pray that I can have more of them. In most of them, Marge has appeared to be about as old as she was when we first started dating. She has always been smiling, just as she did on earth, and appeared very happy. Out of these three experiences, I only remember Marge talking in the second one, when she told me we had to get back to answer the phone. Each time I have had an experience, the thing I remember most is a beauty beyond human description. In my last two experiences, we seemed to be flying gracefully, just kind of coasting along. In the first one, I flew at a very high rate of speed to get to Marge.

To the One I Love — part 8

We try each day to look for our purpose

We look very hard, but the reasons don't surface

We learn to treat people with love and respect

We hope in God's eyes we're doing what is correct

The road to Heaven is so full of sorrow

After each life problem, we pray for a better tomorrow

Tomorrow never comes, so we live for today

With guidance from above, we will find the way

Then, someday we will see a glimmer of light in the distance

We will move toward the light with little resistance

The light in the sky is like a magnet calling for us

We will head for the light, for in God we do trust

I love you — Nim

On the nights that I have had out-of-body experiences, my dog has sat and growled softly while staring at what I assume is a spirit. Most of the times that Ellie has done so, I have had a good experience during the night. I look forward to seeing Ellie stare at something and growl softly, and try to fall asleep as fast as I can.

Our trip to Canada was a lot of fun, but I would give the rest of it for another trip like I had with Marge. People that have had out-of-body experiences understand the beauty that is beyond explanation. Imagine the best thing you have ever had happen, and multiply the feeling of self-fulfillment by thousands.

Chapter 24

Happy Birthday

July was there, and my birthday was approaching very quickly. I did not have any special plans for my birthday, so I just worked as usual. While I was in the shower, I heard Marge start singing "Happy Birthday" in my head. I didn't want anyone at work to know it was my birthday, but a couple of ladies that have birthdays close to mine remembered and I had people calling me on the phone all day, singing "Happy Birthday." All through the day, Marge kept singing to me in my head.

It had been over nine months since Marge departed and I missed her every day. I think how great it is that I have all the contact that I do with her in the spirit world. Naturally, I miss her physically, but I still hear her giggle, and she talks to me a lot. Like a talented singer or a very sick person might ask *Why me?*, I can say *Why me to be given this gift?* This gift is great to have, especially on my really down days.

To the One I Love – Part 9

This wonderful gift that I have been given

Makes my life still so worth living

Communication with my wife after she has been gone

Is so wonderful, it's like a beautiful song

I don't know why I was given this wonderful skill

Or whatever you call it, it sure is a thrill

Gifted psychics can talk with the dead

I get my communication from a voice in my head

It's so great to hear Marge talk to me

It helps a lot to deal with my misery

I love you — Nim

I went fishing with my friend and ended up buying a used camper that was sitting at the campground. It was very old, but the previous owner had just refinished the whole interior. Like my wife, he had passed on from cancer a few months prior. It was a nice little getaway place for my dog and I. Ellie became quite accustomed to the place; she would run from end to end looking out the windows to watch for dogs. She barked too much so we had to put a bark collar on her. It was not the type that shocks the dog; instead, it puts out a citronella spray that dogs dislike. She learned to behave with the collar on, so we could leave for a couple hours at a time to go shopping or fishing. It wasn't long before she had dog bones hidden all over the camper.

The previous owner had paid the lot rental fee, so we decided to get a lot of use out of the camper that summer. We stayed there for fishing tournaments and for leisure weekends. My son and his friend went up there, and so did my other son and I. We had a lot of fun, and it made the summer go by quickly.

Then, one night at about two in the morning, Ellie was growling softly and I figured someone was walking outside. When I looked up, I saw what people would describe as a ghost walking away from me down the hallway. It was gone immediately, and I lay awake for quite a long while to see if it would return. It did not return, and I didn't say anything to my son about it. The figure was much too large to be that of Marge. For some reason, it looked like a male — a quite large male. At this time, I haven't found out if the previous owner who passed on was a large man. I hope to find out this summer.

I have read between fifteen and twenty spiritual books, and a couple talked about lost souls and ghosts. For quite a while, I thought that maybe Marge was a lost soul, but I obtained proof later that she was not. I have read about ghosts, and that they will do you no harm. One book said to just tell them to go and they will leave. I felt that maybe she had stayed behind to help me cope with her loss, and had not crossed over. I really felt bad that I might have kept her from going to the light. I read in a couple of books that you have to let go of your loved ones at some time. So as I cried last spring after my Vegas trip, I told Marge I was letting her go and she could move on.

She said, "No, you are not ready for that yet."

I tossed that idea around in my head for quite a while, thinking she was here just for me; then I read in another book that some very spiritually advanced souls could visit quite often. I was getting more and more confused, but remained happy with all the contact that I had with the spirit world. I became so euphoric at times that I wanted to join her right away. I knew suicide was not the answer, however, so I realized I was stuck on this earth until my time is up, and if I have to be here, I am going to make the best of it.

I started to write a book years ago to talk about the light and how my urge for drinking had been lifted. All of a sudden I have had all this contact with my wife, so I thought I would continue writing and see where it goes. The rest of the summer, I had contact with Marge talking in my head. Sometimes she would start talking at the weirdest times. I love it when she comes to me in a store and I just start laughing. People look at me like I'm crazy. I might be the only person who thinks differently, but I know that I'm not.

Chapter 25

Fishing and Hunting

The early fall was here, which meant great fishing and a fishing tournament to participate in. It is quite an honor to catch a muskellunge and have your name placed on the board. My son Brian and I had accomplished that several times throughout the years; in 1998, we caught three fish and took second place. That is quite a feat when you have 200 boats out pounding the water. Muskellunge are called the fish of 10,000 casts, and sometimes it seems like they take many more casts than that. The year Brian and I took second place, we won $5,000; amazingly, the first place team was from our cottage. We happened to chose the right lake and cast the right baits that year. Also, I had missed a fish that would have brought us 1st place and a check for $15,000 instead. The thing that made it all the much better was that all the fish we boated were caught on bait that I had made.

Years prior, when I quit drinking, I'd started a hobby of making baits to use up some of my time. It is a great feeling when you make your own bait and actually catch fish on it. I have probably caught between 50 – 75 musky on my homemade buck tails since I started making them. I was selling them in sporting goods stores until I got sick of the shop owners trying to talk me down in price; now I just make them for a few friends and family.

Brian and I fished the same set of lakes as we had for several years. In this tournament, there are four groups of lakes to choose from, and once you pick you are limited to those lakes. Shortly after we started, I had a big musky strike, and after I had set the hook, he began to fight. I lost him a short time later, and when I looked at my watch, it was 8:17 a.m. I missed another fish later, and when I looked at my watch, it was 11:17 a.m. If I had caught those two fish, we would have been in the money again. Throughout the tournament, I heard Marge talking in my head; just like magic, when I turned the radio on, one of our favorite oldies songs was playing. The next day, we didn't have any luck, either, but we did have a good time. When fishing for musky, you have to be quite patient, but when you hook into one it is quite a thrill. After fishing, we headed back home, 200 miles away, to get ready for work on Monday.

Bow Hunting Season

Bow hunting season was upon us once more

Time to sit in a tree stand and try to score

I sat in my tree stand thinking about my past

Wondering how long the sorrow could last

It was so relaxing watching the squirrels gather their food

Just watching nature helped lift up my mood

I was watching the water flow slowly down the creek

Waiting for a buck to come by on the sneak

Relaxation is a key to help heal my grief

Sitting in a quiet woods brings some relief

These quiet times help me so very much

It's a time for my wife and I to keep in touch

After returning from fishing musky in northern Wisconsin, it was time to start bow hunting for whitetail deer. It was time to see if all the work we had done, building food plots and planting trees, was doing any good at keeping the deer on our land. One day, while I was walking out to my stand, Marge began talking and telling me how well all the little pine trees were growing. I am quite used to her talking to me by now, but I enjoy every time she does. It is just another assurance that she is doing fine on the other side. As I sat in my tree, I let my mind wander; I thought back on my beliefs and how I had changed in the last eleven months, and even more since farther back. Since 1972, the year my mother passed away and my brother was killed, I'd chosen to believe in nothing, but I had been brought up as a Lutheran and went to Sunday school and church weekly. Back then, I believed that if you believed in God and prayed, after you died you would be put in the ground, until one day you would be judged and then either go up to Heaven or down to hell.

Before I was married, I became a Catholic, and went to church as often as I could. Then, when my brother was killed, I quit believing. I continued to think about how one night in alcohol treatment I had gone down on my knees and started praying, and then was surrounded by light and saw a face that reminded me of George Washington. I also felt a slight touch on my shoulder, and without hearing any voice, I was told that my urge for drinking had been lifted. From that time on, I believed there must be something of a God of some kind to answer our prayers.

Now, here it was 2005; my wife had passed on almost a year ago, and I knew there was eternal life on the other side. Marge had proven that to me on numerous occasions. I saw a couple deer too far away to shoot, and I was just enjoying the tranquility of the evening, anyway. As darkness was nearing, I looked toward the sky, closed my eyes, and said, "Where are you, Marge?" When I opened them again, I saw thousands of little lights in front of my eyes. Where these little lights came from, I can only suspect, but I was talking to Marge right before they lit up. It was like a fireworks show just for me from my wife.

My Special Light Show

Another month and another poem
For the nonbelievers I will try to show them
I needed a sign and you lit a thousand tiny lights
Once again, I knew you were all right
Life on earth is over in a very short while
Treat everyone with love and then leave in style
Our lives are judged by the people we touch
So treat people kindly and show you love them so much
When you judge yourself at the life review
You will be smiling, not feeling blue

There have been several times that I have had these little light shows, and until proven differently, I have to believe Marge has something to do with them. Several times that I went bow hunting, I felt Marge's presence around me. One day in late October, it was very windy, so I sat in one of the stands that we used for rifle hunting. It was really too windy to hunt deer, but my son and I had made plans, and we said we were going to sit all day. I was prepared with a spiritual book and a backpack of food and drinks. I had opened a can of soda and was preparing to have a sandwich when I dropped my book to the floor. I challenged Marge, and said, "If you have all that power, let me see you move my book."

Just as I said that, the wind died to nothing and my soda can went flying. As I chuckled to myself, my bow, which had been placed across the corner so it wouldn't fall, came sliding toward me. I was totally amazed that my bow moved that much, yet stayed on top of the box I was sitting in. Just as quick as the wind had stopped, it picked up again, and was very strong. I didn't even see if the book moved because I had been so intrigued by the soda can flying and my bow moving. What stopped the wind for that couple of seconds is a mystery to me, but I am sure that Marge made the can fly and the bow move. After she did it, I could hear her familiar giggle in my head. I have had just too many things happen to call them coincidence. For people who have had experiences with the deceased, it is easy to believe all the things that happened to me. People who have not had any of these types of experiences seem to doubt that there is an afterlife and that we can communicate with our loved ones.

One Year into Eternal Life

We wander through life, our bodies on fire

Finding our soul mate is our only desire

Once we have found them, we set a new pace

We slow down to enjoy life; it is no longer a race

We walk very slowly, holding each other's hands

As we work daily on life's many demands

As we have children, our lives start to gain speed

We are going everywhere fulfilling our children's needs

As we grow older, we slow down the pace

Life is so precious, it's no longer a race

Life then ended for my beautiful bride

The rest of my life I will now take in stride

I love you — Nim

I did a lot of bow hunting, and put in a lot of work on a little 12'x12' hunting shack. Keeping busy was the only thing that helped me to deal with the loneliness. I enjoyed my time in the woods and the special conversations I had with Marge. I passed up on shooting many small bucks because I had one big one that kept coming near, but not near enough to get a good shot. We practice "quality deer management," which only allows us to shoot the bigger bucks in addition to taking several does out of the herd.

There were several times that I was sitting in my tree stand thinking of Marge, when a shooting star would shoot across the sky. This happened several times while I was waiting for it to get light in the morning.

November 13, 2005

Today would have been Marge's 54th birthday. It is amazing how fast time is going. My sister Donna called and asked what that number was that I always talk about. I asked her why, and she told me about asking Marge if she was still around to give her a sign. Donna said in the middle of the night, her light came on in her bedroom. She said she looked at her digital clock, and it was 3:17. I told her yes, it was the number 17 that always came up in my life.

Donna went on to tell me that the light in her bedroom had a switch that had to be turned for the light to come on. Donna didn't know how to tell her husband, Butch, what had happened, because she thought he would think she was nuts. At the breakfast table, Butch said, "We have a ghost in our house; the light in our bedroom went on in the middle of the night."

Donna had had an experience shortly after Marge passed, while sitting in a room where she and Marge used to sit and drink coffee. Donna said that she was sitting, thinking about Marge, and she looked across the street and saw the most beautiful emerald-green light coming out of the sky and through the tree down to the ground. She said there was no explanation for the emerald light, and she never saw it again. When the light in her bedroom went on, it scared Donna, and she unplugged the light. I told her, "You asked for a sign and got one — what more do you want?" She finally plugged the light back in, after a couple months had gone by. I did have one experience that scared me, which I will talk about later.

To the skeptic: How could anyone argue about afterlife with so many experiences happening, and happening with a couple of different people? If I had any doubt about an afterlife (which I definitely didn't, after four people came to me in a vision), I certainly don't now. Skeptics could claim we were making things up. Well, the people that associate with me know I am a quite honest person, and I sure wouldn't make up stories about the deceased. It is a shame that some people do make up stories about this type of thing just to make money.

I used to be quite skeptical myself until a few years ago, when my friend's little boy was killed in a car accident. Another friend of mine told me to buy him a specific book about a lady who died, went to Heaven, and then came back to life and wrote about her experience. I bought two copies of the book and read one before I gave a copy to my friend. It was so remarkable that I read the whole book in one afternoon. I have actually read the book three times already. I gave a copy of it to my wife to read, and she asked if I was preparing her for death. I told her no, but it was a very interesting subject and would take up some of her time, being sick at home anyway.

Since that book, I have read about twenty other books dealing with spirits and the afterlife. I've had so many things happen to me exactly as I read later in these books, that now I am totally convinced of the afterlife.

I have a friend at work who seems to doubt the things I say, but he has no proof to offer that is contrary to my beliefs. In one of the books, it said that people who have had these experiences intuitively seek out other people who have had similar experiences. I worked overtime just a couple of days ago, and felt secure enough to talk about some of my experiences with a coworker. He was so happy that I

123

mentioned it to him, and went on to tell me about one he'd had. His sister who lived out on the West Coast came to him at the time of her death to show him she was all right. She passed on from cancer, as my wife did. At first, the times didn't work out, until he remembered to compensate for the time zone changes. Just estimating, I would say that over eighty percent of the people I've felt confident enough to talk to about my experiences either had one or more themselves, or knew someone who had. To me that is more than ample proof of the afterlife.

There will always be some skeptics out there that want to debate the fact of afterlife, but for me, it gives me hope that I will see my loved ones again. How could I feel any other way after all of the contact I have had — not just with my wife, but with other loved ones, also? I can't explain how some of these things happen, but I am very happy they do. On many occasions, they have brought a smile to my face or a chuckle to make my day much more livable.

Chapter 26

Big Buck

The Wisconsin gun season arrived, and was the first time in a long time that we have had snow on the ground for opening day. As I sat in my mini house on stilts, I could see two bucks fighting an hour before opening time. They were quite easy to make out with the snow for a background and the moon for a light. As the dark was disappearing and a new morning coming, I saw a large doe standing on a scrape, waiting for a mate.

The older I get, the more comfortable I want to be while hunting, so I have a stand with a roof, walls, and windows and a little propane heater inside. I hadn't even started my Mr. Heater yet, as opening time was fast approaching. About one minute after the season had officially opened, I shot a big buck and my season was over. It was an eight-point buck with an over sixteen-inch inside spread, which I was quite proud of. When my son came over, he told me it was the buck he had passed up while bow hunting a few weeks previous. He'd wanted to shoot one with over a 20-inch spread so that is fine with me.

Having been an avid deer hunter all of my adult life, I am loosing the urge to kill deer. I just enjoy the outdoors more and more each year. This was just another day that Marge continuously talked in my head. She talked to me about the hunting land and the wild berries that she couldn't wait to be ready the year before. When they finally had been ready, we picked a half a bucketful, but I knocked them out of the refrigerator onto the floor. I don't know why (probably the stress I was under, with Marge's illness at the time), but I never thought of washing them — I just threw them away.

Shortly after we loaded our deer on the truck, I became very ill. Brian had shot a nice buck and a doe. I'd also had to pass up one of the biggest bucks I'd ever seen because I didn't have a deer tag left. I became so ill that I just couldn't wait to get home. I lay on the couch for about fifteen hours and woke up feeling good enough to go to work.

On Thanksgiving Day, it hit me again, and I was back on the couch. I don't remember ever being so sick in my life. As I was on the couch half-asleep, I remember talking to Marge and telling her that I was ready to come by her. I don't think she answered me, but I continued to have visions of her in my dreams, as though she was watching over me. I have a very arthritic back, and when I become ill, the pain intensifies. It was as though Marge was watching over me while I lay on the couch ready to die. I couldn't drink or eat anything. I didn't have any of the normal flu symptoms; I was just hot and cold and aching all over and wanted to die.

It didn't happen; I guess I wasn't as bad as I thought, and after four days, I got up off the couch and began eating and drinking again. I thought I was much sicker than I was, but I had no fear of death like I used to have. All of the experiences I have had with Marge make death much more acceptable to me. I want to live and watch my children succeed in life and be here to guide them, but the fear of death is gone.

One More Time

Oh, how I long for one more embrace
I reach out to find it, but it's an empty space
It would be so great, just one more kiss
I wouldn't be sitting here, lonely like this

If I had one wish and got a choice
It would be one more time to hear your voice
Just to see your gleaming smile
Would again make my life worthwhile
I would hold you tight and never let go
That would be how my true emotions would show
Just one more time, that's all that I ask
I know I could make the good feelings last

Chapter 27

Holidays

Another Christmas was fast approaching, and again I had no desire to go shopping. I put up my little tree and a couple decorations. I looked at tote after tote of decorations that used to hang throughout our house at Christmas, but I didn't even know where to start. That had been Marge's time of the year, and she enjoyed putting up all the decorations. I managed to get out and do all my shopping in one afternoon, and as soon as I got home, I wrapped all the presents, so that was taken care of, too.

I was working on the storage room, putting up drywall and a new floor, and I wanted to get it finished before Christmas. One day when I was in that room, I smelled the perfume Marge used to wear very distinctly. This, I read in a book written by Dianne Arcangel, is called *olfactory*. I looked all over my bedroom, which adjoined this room, and could not find a trace of her perfume.

I was fast approaching every type of encounter with the deceased possible. I had been on three out-of-body experiences; I had four visual apparitions appear (like a mist, yet I could distinctly see who the faces were); I had heard Marge whisper to me; and I had heard her voice in my head almost daily for quite some time now. I had also seen a picture fly off the shelf; I've had my television turned on, lights turned on, and several times when I was thinking about Marge, the phone would ring once, but nobody would be on the line. I had balloons that were out of helium taken from my hand and lifted high into the sky. I have had my CD in my car turn on, playing my favorite song, and also had the door lock unlocked on my car when I locked the keys inside by accident. I have heard Marge giggle, and also shake my waterbed. For me this is way more proof than is needed to prove there is an afterlife. I have been blessed with a special connection to the spirit world, and I love it. I have had people ask me if these things scared me, and I said, "Of course not. It's my wife who is communicating with me." Some people probably do think I'm nuts, but that is okay, because I know the things that have happened, and it doesn't bother me if some people don't believe me. I just want to help people who have lost loved ones realize that there is an afterlife.

I started going to the pain clinic to try to relieve some pain in my arthritic back. At the clinic, you see a pain doctor, a physical therapist, and a psychiatrist. The doctor seemed quite jovial, the therapist was nice, and then I had to see the psychiatrist. He looked over my file and then commented on how long I had been sober. I told him that while in treatment, I had been surrounded by a light and had the urge to drink lifted from me. He then said, "Huh, you can believe anything you want, I guess, as long as it works."

I am an honest person and I don't like to have anyone try to belittle me or doubt my word. I felt there were many ways he could have gotten his point across without the sarcasm. I knew from that minute on we were going to have a problem. He was probably lucky he hadn't met me in my drinking days, with his attitude. Alcohol treatment did a lot to help me deal with anger, but I still have to work quite hard at it at times. I don't think working in a prison helps much, with all the negative attitudes around me. The negativity seems to rub off on the staff at times. I was a little angry already, because I was missing a lot of overtime. I could have worked if I didn't have appointments two or three times a week. I did want the treatment, however, hoping that it would help my back, so I continued to go.

Christmas was about here and my back was pretty much the same as the day I walked into the pain clinic.

Merry Christmas

The leaves have all fallen and winter is here

The streets are now filling with that holiday cheer

Everywhere I go, I'm surrounded by Christmas spirit

I just can't find it, not yet, but I'm getting near it

I think of the holidays I spent with my wife

I can't get used to it, it's a different life

I will go through the motions and pretend it's all right

But I still think of Marge, all day and all night

When my prayers are said and I drift off to sleep

I hope Marge will join me, if just in a dream

I made it through Christmas Eve at my house, and worked Christmas day from 6 a.m. until 2 p.m. I then went over to my in-laws' to spend some holiday time with them. I wanted to get to talk to my father-in-law, even though he had been too sick to recognize me the last time I was there. He was 97 years old and had cancer, so I couldn't expect too much. He was sleeping and I was lonely, so I took a little drive over to our hunting land, about 15 minutes away. It was well worth it, because I saw one of the most beautiful bucks I had ever seen on our land.

When I got back to my in-laws', my father-in-law was sitting up, waiting for me to return. He wanted to talk to me before he went back to bed. We talked and laughed for a little while, and then he went back to bed, where he was spending most of his time now. He was a great man who had raised nine wonderful children, and I was totally blessed to have been married to his daughter for over 32 years. Thirty-two years was great, but he had been married 66 years — wow! This was the last time that I saw my father-in-law alive. I was glad that we had our little talk and I could have good memories of him, instead of having to watch another death.

The New Year was here, and I was just glad to be finished with the holidays; they are supposed to be cheerful, but that is hard to do when you are missing a loved one. Marge said "Happy New Year!" to me in my head, and I hoped this would be a better year for our family than the last couple.

I was working in the little room I was remodeling, and I again smelled Marge's perfume. It just totally amazes me how that can happen. After a couple of weeks, I finally finished that room and started to move loaded totes back into it.

January went by quite quickly, and Marge talked to me almost daily. It is really funny that if I am looking at a lady and have thoughts, Marge will slightly raise her voice and say, "Nimmy," just as she would have here on earth.

Dianne

I wanted to know more about the afterlife

I wanted to know what had happened to my wife

I read a book named Afterlife Encounters

I wanted to know what the afterlife would amount to

A lot of my questions were answered, that's for sure

The life after earth will be serene and so pure

As we shed our human body, which is needed while here on earth

Our soul continues to Heaven, given a new birth

I tried to contact Dianne by email
Never thinking the contact with her could fail
I then found her address and wrote her a letter
Hoping chances of contacting her would be much better
She received my letter and a friendship did start
We emailed daily until her job caused her to depart
Dianne spends her life helping people who are grieving
Reading the book she wrote was just so relieving
I pray that our friendship will last forever
I don't want it to end; never, never

Chapter 28

Anger

I don't know what it was, but I was having a very bad problem with anger. I kept tripping over the dogs and yelling at them; nothing seemed to be going right for me. I was not using my people skills at work like normal. If inmates irritated me, I would raise my voice and try to belittle them. I was just angry at the world. I hadn't had a stretch of anger like this since my drinking days, and I didn't like it, but couldn't control it either. February 9, 2006, is a night I will never forget. I went to bed like usual, and during the night, I had my fourth out-of-body experience. I was with Marge and we went for a trip. She never said a word to me, but she smiled like normal at me.

She again was the age that she was when we met — which I'd always thought was 18, until her sister pointed out that she had been 17 when I met her. We used to have an 18-year-old drinking age, and the night I met her, she had snuck into the tavern. The bartenders didn't check identification cards too closely on pretty girls like Marge. I know this because I was a bartender at that time.

When we reached our destination, a very tall guy in a robe that touched his toes said, "Do you know where you are?"

I answered, "No," as I was amazed by the enormous number of books I could see. They stretched as high and as far as I could see.

The man in the robe was looking at a book and told me, "You are at the Hall of Life Review." I have read in other books where this is called the "Hall of Records." I was so astonished by being with Marge again, I might have misunderstood exactly what he said. I was totally baffled by the enormous number of books and the surrounding beauty. All the colors seemed to have much greater definition and brilliance. It seemed as though there were hundreds of different colors just in the vicinity I was in. I remember wondering how big a ladder they must have to reach the very high books, and then I realized I must have died. I was somewhat happy to be with Marge, but I felt I had some unfinished business on earth.

Just as I thought that, the man in the robe told me, "You have an anger problem to work on before you come see me again." I kind of chuckled to myself, because I had been having such an issue with anger. I have since figured out that my anger was related to the fact that I'd interrupted taking my antidepressants like they were prescribed.

I awoke again in my bed, with wonderful memories of Heaven. I don't remember much of it, except for the millions of books and wondering how big a ladder they must have needed to reach all the books. One other thing I remember is that I felt like I was at home. Each time I have had one of these experiences, my next day has been great. I feel like I don't have a problem in the world; I love everyone and life is just great. I wish I could choose when to have these experiences, which would probably be every night. The peace and tranquility is so enormous that it is beyond description.

I don't know why I knew I had unfinished business on earth, or for what reason. I guess one reason was that I really wasn't dead, as I had thought. Perhaps one of the reasons was to write this book and give people hope, and help them deal with their grief when they lose a loved one. There are a lot of spiritual books to read and I gain hope in each one I read. All of the experiences I'm writing about have happened to me. Hopefully they will help to prove to people that there truly is an afterlife. I feel free to talk about them because I know I am telling the truth, and if people don't want to believe me, they will learn when they get there. I have only one friend who seems to doubt my word; he doesn't come right out and say it, but I can tell by the looks I get when I talk about my experiences.

Just the other day, I was working overtime, sitting in a hospital with an inmate who was having continual seizures, when I started talking to the other officer about my experiences. She was so happy; she told me that her deceased brother talks to her all the time, but she was afraid to tell anyone for fear they wouldn't believe her. I had mentioned earlier that I worked with a guy whose sister came to him at the time she passed, and she lived several states away. I think most people are afraid to talk of their experiences because they fear people will doubt their word.

I try to live every day with love and respect for everyone that comes into my life. It is very hard to do, especially working in a prison with some of society's worst human beings. I try to treat them with respect, no matter what their crimes were. I don't usually want to know what they are in for, because I don't think I can condone child molesters, rapists, or some other crimes. I do want to know their crimes, however, if I am transporting them to a hospital, just to see if they have a record of assault or liking to run. I try to treat them all decently, which is quite a challenge, especially while I was dealing with my anger problem.

Hall of Life Review

We were racing across Heaven with Marge in the lead

I had no directions, I didn't have a need

I stayed behind, wondering what our destination would be

I stayed close behind her, for ahead I could not see

I wondered and wondered where we were going

Marge looked back and smiled, I knew I'd be shown

We arrived at a place surrounded by books
We were met by a man in a robe, with Heavenly looks
He looked at me and said, Do you know where you are?
I said no, I'm lost so far
He said you are at the Hall of Life Review
I thought I was dead, my life, was through
He said, you have a problem with anger, it's easy to see
Go back and work on it, before you come back to see me
I woke up at home in my own bed
I was still alive, I was not dead

Chapter 29

Another Death

February went by very quickly, with my almost daily visits from Marge. Her dad was becoming very sick, and I just couldn't go to see him anymore. I'd had a good little chat with him on Christmas, and that was how I wanted to remember him. In his last couple days, he kept talking about how Marge was there to take him to the light. He kept wondering where Bernie was. Bernie was his son who had been killed in an accident when he had driven under a semi with his pickup truck. I had read in several books that sometimes when people have traumatic deaths, their souls get lost on earth. I told Marge's family about what I had read, and we all thought perhaps that is what had happened to Bernie.

A while back, I read a wonderful book, written by Dianne Arcangel, titled *Afterlife Encounters*. I tried to email her, but it came back to me. Persisting, I wrote her a letter with some questions I had about the afterlife and all my experiences with Marge. Much to my amazement, she emailed me back, and we started to have a good email relationship. Dianne has some very exceptional credentials in afterlife encounters studies, among them being the former directorship of the Kubler-Ross Center of Houston; she was also on the board of directors for the Rhine Research Center and the National Institute for Discovery Science. I felt if anyone could answer some of my questions, she could.

One morning a couple days before Marge's dad's passing, I was looking out my kitchen window trying to see if I could contact Marge; she told me she was busy. When I emailed Dianne and told her my wife had told me she was busy, she was as happy as could be. I had never been told by Marge that she was busy before, however, I didn't think much of it, knowing her father was about to pass. As a matter of fact, I thought it might be common to have a lost loved one tell you that.

Dianne said she had danced around the idea of the deceased being busy for several years. She said that one of her researchers had told her to never tell anyone that their loved ones were too busy to be with them. She said I made her day, her week, and her month. I was so happy that I had helped someone who did so much to help grieving people. I helped confirm the fact that the deceased do have things to do on the other side. Although I have not yet met her, I will always have a special spot in my heart for Dianne.

Marge's dad was 97 years old, and battled to the very end, which I think he did because he wondered where his son Bernie was. His family thinks that maybe he hung on until the first of March so his wife wouldn't have to send any Social Security money back. Marge's dad passed peacefully on March 1, 2006, exactly 17 months to the day after his daughter Marge passed on. As soon as he passed on, I wrote a poem from him to his family.

I asked Marge about Bernie, and she said that he was lost; he was still on earth. She said, "We have to get him up; we have to get him over here. Yes, Daddy is with me now. I am kind of overjoyed to be with Dad again. Now we can work on Bernie together, to get him to come to the light by us. Dad is better now, and doesn't have cancer anymore. Dad is all smiles. Nimmy, I've got to go now; we have some things to do. We have to get ready for the funeral." I don't know what Marge and her Dad had to do to get ready for the funeral, but in one of the books I read, it stated that the deceased can chose to attend their funerals if they want to.

To Ruth, my wonderful wife of 66 Years, all of our children, relatives, and friends

It was seventeen months ago today

The good Lord took our daughter away

One thing I never did quite understand

Was how I outlived two children that were both so grand

It goes to show God has a plan

When our time comes, we leave this land.

I looked up and saw Marge's gleaming smile

And I knew it was time to leave just for a while

We are now at a place that is full of light

Everything around us is glowing so bright

From Henry (Hank) Gawel

Written by my son-in law, Nim

The day that I wrote that poem, my son Brian and I were going to go to our hunting land to cut some firewood for our camper. Brian told me he had to run back into the house and get a sweatshirt, and I sat in the truck. All of a sudden, I heard the very distinct voice of Hank say, "Thank you, Nim, for the beautiful poem. It was so nice for you to think of me and write that very special poem." I couldn't believe it, that I was having contact with Marge's dad already. He had just passed away earlier in the morning. It was just plain remarkable, and I almost felt guilty because he had came to me first. However, I felt very honored because Marge's father was a very religious and a very special man to many.

March 2, 2006

After I awoke in the morning and got in the shower, Marge began talking to me again in my head. I told her I missed her, and she said not to worry, that we will all be together again and it will be a big reunion. I asked her if she ever saw my family, and she told me yes, all the time. She said my father is all smiles just like he was on earth, and that they all have jobs. She said they were still working on Bernie, but he was going to come over to the light. I don't know how or why I have this special means of communication with Marge, but I love it. She must have taught her dad how to communicate already, as he had thanked me for the poem I wrote for him yesterday. Wow, I just love the communication with my loved one and her father.

A couple days later, we spent the afternoon and evening at the funeral home. They displayed the poem I had written, and I received several compliments for it. Most people, including myself, didn't believe I had the talent to write poetry. My daughter thinks I should write a poem that doesn't rhyme. I will work on it. To me, way back when I was in school and they made us write poetry, all I ever learned was poetry that rhymed.

While we were at the funeral home, Marge's brothers and sisters and myself had a discussion about Bernie and why he didn't show up to help bring his dad over to the light. I told them what I thought, and that Marge had talked in my head and said that Bernie would come over. I was somewhat in awe that all of the family listened so intently and believed all that I said. I guess they knew I was quite an honest man, especially after I had quit drinking years before.

I then talked to one of my sisters-in-law, and we began to exchange stories about visits from the deceased. She told me many stories about her son, who passed away shortly after Marge had. She talked of one time she knew her son was present, and she told him to poke the dog in the butt. She said a couple seconds later, her dog spun around to see what had touched him. I was so happy that someone I knew was having the same type of experiences I was. It was like I finally had someone I could relate to.

I had written Dianne an email asking if she thought that the deceased could coax a spirit that was stuck on earth over to the light. I don't think Dianne had received my email telling her that Marge's dad passed away. I got an email asking if Marge's dad had passed on yet. That night I read in a book that deceased could actually coax spirits that were stuck on earth to go to the light. That was good to know, because Marge had told me that Bernie would come over to the light.

While I was driving home from the funeral home, I was talking to my oldest son, Brian, on my cell phone, telling him how Marge had told me that Bernie would come over to the light once his dad got there. Right after I talked to Brian, Marge started talking in my head; all of a sudden, she raised her voice and said, "Bernie's over."

Out of all the times that Marge had talked to me, I never once can remember when she raised her voice when telling me something. I am sure she was excited, because she quit talking to me right then and there. I was happy for her family, and quickly called one of Marge's sisters to relay the message to the rest of the family. I think he just needed that little extra coaxing of having his dad at the light to get him to go over. It really makes me wonder how hard Marge worked to try to coax Bernie over. Now, all three of them are over, and just waiting for the rest of us to come to the light.

Coaxing Bernie

Marge passed and came to escort her dad

Bernie wasn't there, and her father was quite sad

Marge told me Bernie would come to the light

Once their dad arrived, he would give up the fight
While driving back from the funeral home in the early night
Marge talked in my head and told me Bernie had come to the light
A few years had passed since Bernie left
He died in an accident, his truck was all messed
Marge had a tough time dealing with the loss of her brother
I had lost a brother, father, and mother
I tried to console her as she had done for me
It wasn't easy, for the time it just couldn't be
We all deal with loss in different ways
For some it takes years, others just days

Beauty

Our earth is filled with beauty, a magnificent sight
According to Marge, it's nothing compared to the light
The beauty of Heaven, she can't explain
There are all kinds of animals roaming the plain
I have been there at night just for a visit
The only words to explain it are purely magnificent
There's beauty on earth with each new creation
The beauty of Heaven has no explanation
Once we've succumbed to our earthly fate
We will start our trip of beauty by going through the gate

I woke up early on March 5th, the day of Marge's dad's funeral. I drove to Beaver Dam to pick up some things at the store, and on my way back, I was going to stop at the cemetery where Marge is buried. As I was driving down the road getting ready to turn to go to the cemetery, I was wondering why I had all the contact with Marge and even her dad but none with my family. My father, brother, mother, and grandmother had appeared in a vision, but they had not talked to me.

All of a sudden, my father started talking to me. He said, "Jimmie, we'll all here having fun, and we all have a job, but you have work to do on earth yet." He then chuckled as he would have on earth and said, "You have a lot of fish to catch yet." It was definitely my father talking to me after all these years. I emailed Dianne and told her about my father coming to talk to me, and she wondered what he'd said. I told Dianne that he had passed in 1989, and she said, "Oh, 17 years ago." I chuckled because there was my 17 again. I then went on to tell her what he had said. I sometimes wonder if he had tried to communicate other times, and I just thought it was all in my head.

My family and I went to the funeral to pay our last respects to my father-in-law. There were a lot of relatives there from California and Illinois, a lot of people I hadn't seen in quite a few years. It was nice getting to talk to them, and in a short while, it was all over, and I was back home to live my life again.

<u>Body</u>

Our body is a vehicle to carry our soul

It needs that protection until we reach our goal

We don't know our mission while here on this earth

It was given to each of us secretly at birth

God has a plan and gave us a reason to live

One of the reasons, I'm sure, is to love and to give

Our body was given us not to abuse
And if we abuse it, I'm sure we will lose

It is almost the end of March, 2006, and I continue to work and try to go on with my life. I can't imagine the pain and suffering that people go through who don't have the very special spiritual contact that I do with the spirit world. As I have said before, I don't know why I was chosen to have this special contact with the spirit world. I do feel that part of the mission given to me was to pass on all my experiences and let people know that there definitely is a life after life on earth.

The beauty I have seen during my out-of-body experiences is beyond description. There are no words to explain what I have seen. I wish I could have taken a camera with me. The beauty of Marge was beyond belief. She was a very pretty young lady, and remained pretty all her life, but the times I have gone with her, the beauty of her body is beyond description.

Since all these things have happened, I have a new outlook on life. Some of the things that used to bother me don't bother me at all. I still have a lot to do with working on my anger, but the point is that I am working on it. None of us on earth are perfect, but we must strive to work on our character defects so we can learn unconditional love. It is really hard working in a prison with some of society's worst people. It is hard to treat a child molester with respect. It is hard dealing with some of the inmates, knowing they would just as soon stick a shank in your back as look at you. Evidently, God figured I could handle this mission, because I am two weeks short of 25 years in the prison system.

I sometimes feel bad that I had to be an alcoholic and have chronic back pain, emphysema, and depression. I change my mind on how bad I have it when I look at someone in a wheelchair, someone with seizures, diabetes, or the many other diseases there are.

I have been faced with several financial problems in my life, but I keep on working and hacking away at my bills. Everything works out in the end, I am told, so I shouldn't worry so much about things. I have some friends who are rich, but I don't think their lives are any better than the life that Marge and I had and I continue to have. I have no problem working overtime and giving most of the money to our children. I have all the things in life that I need, not necessarily all the things I would like to have. Then again, if I hadn't made several bad choices in life, like alcohol and gambling, I might have a few more of the things I would like.

I sometimes wonder what life would have been if I had tried harder in school, or gone on to college instead of the Army. Each choice we make can turn our lives in different directions. I wouldn't give the life that I had with Marge and our children up for anything. There were several bad times and many obstacles in life, but we worked at it and never gave up hope. Even to Marge's last breath, we were praying and hoping for that miracle that wasn't meant to be. Marge's mission on earth was complete; I can only guess what her mission was, but I am sure one of them was to straighten me out. I was heading for self-destruction by alcohol; she stuck with me to the end, and for that, I love her very much. I was just so blessed that Marge's friend introduced me to her, and that we went on to have a pretty good marriage.

Chapter 30

Phone Rings

I woke up one morning at the end of March and heard the telephone ringing. When I got to it, it was not making a sound, yet I could still hear a phone ringing. I ran to the hallway where there was a big box; the box had a plastic telephone in it that was doing the ringing. I thought it was quite goofy, because it had a weird ring. When it stopped ringing, I picked it up, shook it, and did everything I could think of, but couldn't get it to make a sound.

<u>Phony Noises</u>

I awoke to the telephone; I could hear it ringing

But when I got to it, it wasn't even dinging

I ran to the hallway and listened for the noise

But all I saw was a box of toys

I looked and saw where the noise had come from

It was so weird and sounds kind of dumb

A little toy phone, made of plastic

Was the culprit, making all the racket

When things like this happen, it's just another sign

I will see my wife again in due time

A few days later, I was cleaning out a storage room filled with old toys that our children accumulated over the years. I heard a noise coming out of one of the boxes of stuffed animals. I picked up the little elephant, but it wouldn't make a noise. When I sat it back down, it made a rattling noise again. The little stuffed elephant was all dirty, and I decided to burn it with all the rest of the junk I had gathered. As I threw it in the burn barrel, it made one last little rattling noise. I almost felt bad for burning it.

As I was typing the paragraph above, I happened to look up at a picture of Marge on the computer shelf, and an artificial plant with flowers, leaves, and a little birdhouse in it began to shake like there was a brisk wind in my computer room. This went on for a few seconds, and then it was still again. Once again, what created the force to make the artificial plant shake so much was unexplainable. All I could think is that Marge is showing me she is all right *just one more time*. There were no fans on or any doors open, nor any other logical reason for the plant to start shaking as though caught in a heavy wind. Needless to say, it was 8:17 p.m. when this happened. The number 17 just keeps popping up all over in my life.

A friend of mine that I work with gave me a printout of angel numbers, and they are as follows:

17 – You're on the right path with your thoughts. You have good reason to be optimistic about your plans and path. This powerful and sacred number also represents the Holy Trinity and pyramids. [She told me it could also be 1 and 7, or 1 + 7, which would be 8.]

1 – This is a binary number; every number is divisible by one. We are all one; thereby we're all associated by thought. Watch your thoughts, and focus on your desires rather than your fears.

7 – You're on the right path; keep up the good work.

8 – Financial abundance is coming to you now.

March 31, 2006

I was in bed and asked Marge if she could come and take me with her again. She said she would see and told me she was quite busy. That night, she came and took me with her on another trip to Heaven. She was wearing the pea-green blouse that her engagement picture was taken in. We were together for a short time, and we merged again like I explained previously. I again had one of my best days since her passing after awaking so refreshed and happy.

I can't really explain what happens in a way that would make any sense to anyone who has never had such an experience. It seemed like we melted together and became one. Whatever happens, I yearn for more. My next day was so upbeat and I was all smiles, which hasn't happened since the last experience where we merged.

Another Trip to Heaven

One night, Marge came and gave me a tug

I knew I would have that one more hug

I was out of my body in Heaven, per se

I followed her lead, she lead the way

She wore her smile and her pea-green blouse

The one I remembered her wearing around the house

The scenery was miraculous from way up above

The feeling I felt was of unconditional love

I could tell by taking one more glance

I would be granted that one more chance

We hugged and merged in a show of love

These wonderful feelings were granted from up above

Nearly each day that passes, I can hear Marge talk in my head. It is great to have knowledge that there is a life beyond. I had my first date since Marge passed, and I could hear Marge encourage me to continue with my life. She wants me to go on and have a good life. She keeps telling me to not worry about money, because it will come and all the bills will be taken care of. If she can see into the future the way it sounds, I'm happy I don't know everything. I don't think life would be too enjoyable if we knew what was going to happen on any given day. However, it is nice to think that all my bills will be taken care of. Until that time, I will continue to work and work a lot of overtime to help pay them.

This is the second poem written by my son Timothy.

Message of Love

A year and a half

Has gone and past

Still not easy

But gone so fast

Sometimes I think all is well

Then I stir my emotions back to Hell

The tears come as the memories go

Why God took her, only He knows

All I ask is for one more word

A hello or goodbye, is that absurd?

I must go on each and every day

With a hole in my heart here to stay

Then something inside tells me to smile

The love of a mother watching over her child

All is well, nothing to fear

A soul at ease, a mind that's clear

I know now what need be done

A gift given from mother to son

On April 7, 2006, Marge came to me and told me to keep writing. I don't know if it will go anywhere or not. I do know that the time I have spent writing has helped me to deal with my grief, and think about my life and what it has meant. I try to figure out what my purpose on this earth is all about. I still have a temper to work on. I have to learn to think things over before I put my anger into words. Usually, the things that get me so angry will be minute in my life after a day or two.

Heaven

I look forward to Heaven after this life

So I can spend eternity next to my wife

When we meet again, it will be a happy day

The feeling of excitement would be too much to say

They say we were in Heaven before coming to earth

We accomplished that mission when we came here by birth

On earth, we learn by the mistakes we make

This is all done for our own sake

While here on earth, we have a mission to do

We will return to Heaven when our mission is through

Each day I face is a new challenge, just going to work and wondering what my day will be. I have chronic back pain, and am on heavy medication for it. I don't like the medication, but every time I try to not take it, I pay. I have had a lot of mood swings since Marge passed on. I get days where I just want to be with her, and other days I just want to live and spend time with my children. I have started dating, and Marge encourages me to go on with my life. She was the type of lady who would want happiness for all her family after she left. I know I will meet her again; she has told me so. I am totally convinced that we go to another life right after the one on earth. I have just had too many things happen to be coincidence. I miss Marge and always will, but I now know I can't just stop living, nor do I want to. Our family is still dealing with addictions, and always will until we have all passed on. We can beat these addictions as long as we seek help.

I look back at dealing with my alcoholism and wonder, "Was it an angel that came to me as light? Was it God that came to me as light?" I can't answer that question, all I know is that I was surrounded by a bright light that didn't hurt my eyes, and I saw a face in the light, I felt a hand on my shoulder, and I had the urge to drink lifted from me on that night. I am forever grateful to the light, whatever it was — it saved my life.

Finding Happiness Again

For a while, I was ready to just cash in

I wanted my afterlife to readily begin

Other than my children, life meant nothing to me

The other side is where I wanted to be

I contemplated ways to make my life end

I didn't think my broken heart would ever mend

I knew it was wrong to think of life termination

Because God had made me his very own creation

Along came a lady who got close to me

She opened my eyes, I could again see

She showed me I could still smile and have fun on this earth

It was as though I was given a new birth

On April 18, 2006, as I was folding underwear, a pair of them was ripped from my hand and ended up on the floor. I could hear Marge's goofy giggle at the time. She just told me again that her giggle is not goofy. Marge knew I hated folding underwear and socks, and I am sure that is why she took the underwear from my hand. I am so happy that things keep happening to let me know Marge is still around, even though these experiences are not as often as before. Most people who have had contact with the afterlife will talk about one or two experiences, but I have had too many to count.

Untitled

As my writing approaches an awaited end

I'm still waiting for my heart to mend

Life is different after all those married years

The moments of true happiness and also the tears

We watched as our children grew up and became adults

*We hoped and prayed for their happiness and also good
results*

We met each challenge life threw our way

We did our best to make each one a happy day

Alcohol recovery had been an emotional ride

We learned to take each challenge in stride

I had been met by a light; the urge for alcohol was lifted from me

It was a great feeling; I was finally set free

We planned to grow old holding each other's hand

It didn't turn out that way; God had a different plan

I still have a lot of contact with voices from Marge, but not quite to the same extent as before. The other night, I was walking in a mall with the lady I'm dating, and Marge told me we made a cute couple. I chuckled and hoped that my friend didn't hear me, but I told her about it the next day anyway. I am not only blessed to have all these experiences with Marge, but also to have a very understanding friend who knows I still have feelings for Marge and always will have them. Having a special friend has put some meaning back into my life. It has taken a lot of the loneliness out, and given me the courage to move forward once again.

I have heard the saying "Everything happens for a reason" a thousand times. I believe that to be true, but I want to know the reason. Why would a little child be killed or beaten? Why would a lady be raped, beaten, or killed? There are so many *whys* that I just can't understand. I don't know why there have to be wars, yet I believe someone has to keep these countries like Iraq and people like Osama bin Laden in line. What could possibly be the purpose of people like Hitler? There are many unanswered questions as I journey on my way to unconditional love. It is quite hard to have any good feelings for a child molester, rapist, or child abuser; however, I deal with that type of person every day working in a prison.

I have walked through life and tried a few different jobs; have spent two years in the military; have smoked for years, then quit; drank excessively for years and entered recovery. I have found that no challenge was insurmountable. I have been a husband for 32 years, and a father for over thirty years. Since recovery began, I have worked hard and tried to do everything in my power to help my children and lead them in the right direction. I have found out that I can preach all I want, but each child has to learn by his or her mistakes. I wish I could take some of the hurt away from my children for the mistakes they make, but that can't happen. They each have to learn by their own mistakes.

I have tried to be the best person I can be and treat all people with unconditional love. It is hard to do, as all people don't act or think alike. Some people are just grouchy, and don't want friends or help from another. I have been blessed with some very good friends. They have lent me an ear when I am down and grieving the loss of my wife. Some have helped me immensely by fixing broken cars, the roof on my house, and several other things. I try to help other people as much as I can, but with my bad back, it is hard to do any physical labor. Sometimes just a few kind words are all someone needs to help make their day. It gives me a great feeling to know that I have helped make someone's day just a little better by a couple of kind words or small good deeds.

Lady Friend

I met a beautiful lady with a great smile

I asked her if she would like to go to Vegas with me for a while

After some persuasion, she agreed to go

We gambled some and went to a show

We walked a lot and did some talking

My hips were sore from all the walking

We had things in common; we had both lost a friend

We needed the time to help our lives mend

The time went by way too fast

I didn't want it to end, I wanted it to last

It was the beginning of a relationship, one full of love

I was again granted a friendship from way up above

Life

What is life? What can it be?

I wonder where it is taking me

I look around, I'm in a daze

My life has changed in so many ways

A young lady came along and steered me straight

A feeling of euphoria, it's all so great

A hand to hold, a body to squeeze

A person to talk to, my anxiety release

A kind smile, a long embrace

I've once again found I still have a place

I look ahead with a grin on my face

I can handle life, I still love this place

Soft Wind

The wind blows softly bringing a cool breeze

The feeling of relaxation puts me so much at ease

I have dealt with grief the best I could

Hoping and praying the rest of my life will be good

Each day in life presents a new challenge

The death of a loved one, there is no revenge
I spend a lot of time with a special lady friend
I hope we stay close until the end
And when the end comes, it won't be so bad
I will reunite with my wife and the love we once had
And when the party on earth is over and we move to the sky
There will be three of us together flying so high

Chapter 31

Ellie

I didn't know where or when to end this book, but I was giving an ending that I did not want. Things still continue to happen with Marge in my life. She still talks to me quite often, and helps me out when I am feeling down. One day when I was donating blood, Marge told me it was good to donate blood because it helped so many people. She told me I should keep donating blood as I have been doing for many years. She continues to tell me not to worry about financial matters, as they will get better in time. Marge tells me to keep writing poetry and continue my life with Pam. I have come to the conclusion that I don't know how I would have handled Marge's passing if I did not have afterlife communication with her. I cannot scientifically prove there is an afterlife or rule out the other explanations for the communication I have had with my loved ones; I have just told the truth the best that I remember, and hope this will help other people deal with the grief of a losing a loved one.

Shortly after Marge passed on in 2004, my children bought me a little pug to keep me company. From the moment I saw her, I knew she was the dog for me. In all my years, I never had a dog of my own. I remembered how as a child, my fathers' dog died, and I felt bad for months and never wanted to deal with that type of loss again, so I'd never gotten a dog of my own. I now had my first puppy at the age of 56. I was a pushover, and right away allowed Ellie to sleep in my bed. She would cuddle up with me and sleep right under my arm. When it was time for me to go to work, Ellie would run down the stairs and wait by the door to be let outside.

Ellie brought so much comfort to me and helped fill the emptiness left by Marge's passing. Several times while I was writing this book and started to cry, Ellie would come running and jump onto my lap and start licking my face until I stopped crying. She could always tell when I was having a rough time, and would do little funny things to make me smile and laugh. I would take her for walks; at 18 pounds, she was the boss of all the animals — her small size didn't matter. I used to laugh because whenever I would get out the leash, she would run so fast in circles that I had trouble getting the leash on her. Ellie loved taking walks, but really loved to go out on my hunting land and run. She also loved going for rides on my four-wheeler ATV. She would ride very contently for hours as I pulled the small plow along, making food plots for the deer.

Every day that I came home from work, Ellie would be lying on the couch looking out the window, waiting for me. She seemed to know just what time it was. When I entered the house, she would run in circles until I let her outside. She would then run to the corner of the fence and bark one time. When she was finished outside, she would come back in and wait for her treat.

My special friend and I started spending a lot of time in northern Wisconsin at the camper I purchased the year before. Ellie loved going out in the boat and watching the fishing lures come through the water. On one occasion, I told my son Tim that if she kept running in the boat, she would end up in the lake swimming. Sure enough, a couple moments later, she tripped on the net and into the water she went. We were laughing so hard, watching her little paws paddling to get her back to the boat. She did manage to fall into the lake a couple more times last summer, so my friend Pam ordered her a doggie life vest. It was hilarious to see her in the bright yellow-green life vest.

The first time Pam put it on her, she didn't seem to like the vest at all. Pam then placed her in the lake, and she took off swimming away from the boat very fast. In a couple seconds, she was about twenty yards from the boat. She then stopped and realized the vest was loose and coming off her head. We could see she was starting to panic, so I tried to get to her using my trolling-motor, but the motor wouldn't work. I was ready to jump into the lake to rescue her when the trolling motor finally worked and we got to her and pulled her into the boat. Ellie had a total look of fear in her eyes, and we realized we had not put the vest on her tightly enough.

The next time we brought Ellie along fishing, we made sure we put her vest on properly. That day, it was so hot out that Ellie was happy to go for a little swim. We had to be careful because the lakes that we fished on had a lot of Muskellunge in them, and they have been known to attack swimming dogs. We hooked a large rope on her and let her swim. She was still a little afraid, but really enjoyed the cool water. Each time Ellie became a little more comfortable having the life vest on, and she enjoyed cooling off in the lake. After a while, she became accustomed to wearing the vest, and she seemed to look forward to going swimming.

On August 17, 2006, I was going to go to my hunting land to gather some firewood for splitting. At first, I wasn't going to take Ellie along, but when I saw how excited she was, I knew I had to take her along. That decision is one I will regret for the rest of my life. As I was loading up the little trailer that I pull behind my four-wheeler, I noticed that Ellie was eating something on the ground. I thought it might be a mushroom, and I yelled for her to come along. I had heard that there are some types of mushrooms that if eaten can be fatal to an animal. Instead of riding on the ATV like usual, Ellie ran all the way back to the road. On the way home, my son Brian drove and Ellie laid on my lap all the way home. That was not unusual, as Ellie was usually quite tired from running on the land. That night, Ellie was acting sick and not her normal playful self. I told Pam to get Ellie into the veterinarian as soon as possible the next morning.

I came home from work early and took Ellie to the vet. I told her I thought Ellie might have eaten a mushroom. She did not think too much about that, and instead gave her a shot for a strained back, and I took her home. I watched Ellie quite closely that night, and noticed she had some darkness in her stool that appeared to be blood. I called in sick to work in the morning and had Ellie at the vet's office as soon as they opened the door. Some people would think I was crazy to use sick leave to tend to my dog, but Ellie was what I came home to and was just like a child to me.

The vet took blood from Ellie and told me to take her to the animal hospital in Appleton, which was about an hour from Waupun. As I was driving and started to think of losing Ellie, I began to cry and veered over the center line, almost hitting a semi head-on. As soon as we got to the hospital, they immediately started to treat Ellie for poison in her system. I told the doctor that I thought it was possible Ellie had eaten a deadly mushroom, and he told me the deadly ones were really rare in Wisconsin. However, he did draw a picture for me of what the deadly type looked like. I then drove home, worrying and crying all the way. I couldn't believe how attached I had gotten to Ellie, and somehow I knew the worst was yet to come.

When I got home, I told Pam how I had almost hit a semi head-on and she wouldn't let me go to my land alone. I wanted to look and see if the area had any mushrooms that looked similar to the picture the doctor had drawn of the deadly mushroom. When we got to my hunting land, I went right to the area where I saw Ellie eating something. We found four different types of mushrooms in a ten-square-foot area. I picked one of each and took them home with me.

When we got home, Brian drove me back to the animal hospital and I took along one that looked like the deadly one the doctor had drawn. The doctor told me he thought it did look like the deadly type, but he had to send it to the University of Wisconsin to have it tested. We were then allowed to visit Ellie in the canine intensive care unit. Ellie was pretty drugged up, but she definitely recognized me. I got to pet Ellie for about half an hour, and I didn't want to leave her. As I walked away, Ellie followed me with her eyes, but didn't even move her head. I just knew this would be the last time I saw her alive. I fought hard to hold back the tears, but a few still trickled down my cheek.

We received a phone call late that night and were asked if I wanted her to have another blood transfusion. I told them to go ahead, but a short time later, we received another phone call and were told that Ellie was in cardiac arrest. Ellie passed on a short time later. I felt as though I had lost another family member. I cried and cried and couldn't imagine life without her. She had brought so much joy and happiness to my life while I was dealing with the loss of my wife, Marge.

I took off work the next day, and went and picked up Ellie to bring her home. I spent the day building her a wooden casket and a cement marker. I carved on top of the marker: "ELLIE, MY BEST FRIEND."

Ellie

When I started the four-wheeler, Ellie would come running

Whether she was watching fish in the creek or just out sunning

She loved being on the four-wheeler, whether plowing or just riding for fun

She would ride along until the work was all done

Every once in a while, she would look up at me

It was getting hot and time for a break under the shade tree

A more playful dog you might never see

I was so happy my children had bought her for me

Sometimes I would hide behind a big tree

Ellie would run in circles looking for me

When Ellie became sick, she lost the distinctive curl in her tail

It was like letting the wind out of a sail

Like when I lost Marge, my life was again put on hold

It will get better with time, so I am told

Ellie was loved so much by my whole family and my friend Pam they all wanted to be present when I buried Ellie. I decided to bury Ellie on my hunting land where she loved to ride the four-wheeler and run around. They say that man's best friend is a dog, and Ellie held up to that standard quite well.

More about Ellie

Ellie knew when I was down, and came to comfort me

She provided laughter endlessly

She made me smile and helped to ease my pain

She made me want to live again

She would run in circles chasing her tail

She tried to catch it, to no avail

She watched TV and got excited about animals on the screen

But horses excited her most by all means

She wasn't very big, yet wanted to be the boss

Now she is big, a very big loss

As I'm here again with my heart full of grief

The fond memories help bring some relief

Now when I lay her down to rest

I remember Ellie, she was the best

It was another of the worst things I ever had to do, when I had to bury Ellie. She was the only dog I have ever had of my own and definitely my favorite. I never wanted to have a dog of my own, in fear that I would become too attached to it, and that is exactly what happened with Ellie. I am happy that I had her to help pull me through some very tough times, but now I have to deal with some very tough times again.

My Best Friend

Anger, anger followed by grief

Each way I turn, there's just no relief

Ellie was the best friend I ever had

That's why her passing leaves me so sad

Each day she waited patiently for me to return from work

I would look at her face and detect a slight smirk

Ellie would snuggle so close to me

In such a short time, she had become family

Ellie would see her reflection and jump back in fear

She just couldn't figure out how she got in the mirror

She did so many things that brought a smile to my face

Now there is emptiness all around this place

The night after Ellie passed on, I was blessed with another out-of-body experience and met with Ellie in the sky. Ellie came running around the edge of the woods headed straight towards me. It was just like the experience that I had with

Marge when we merged. Some studies show that seventy percent of people polled believe that animals have souls. After my experience that night, I am totally convinced that animals have souls. As Ellie ran at me, she appeared to have a smile on her face, and Marge was in the distance smiling at both of us. This was just another experience to show that not only is my wife fine on the other side, but my dog is, too.

Another Experience

I saw trees growing in midair

Ellie came running without a care

Marge was standing off in the distance

I classified it a dream with no resistance

I thought it was funny that Ellie ran on midair

I know I stood there just in a stare

I had out-of-body experiences before

Now I was sure it had happened once more

Ellie is in Heaven by Marge's side

We will all meet again when I take the final ride

I have been very blessed to have so much contact with the other side, and I feel it is my duty to spread the word of my experiences, to perhaps help other people who are grieving the loss of a loved one, human or animal. I am totally convinced that animals do have souls and go to an afterlife just like I believe humans do. Most of my friends believe me, but a few are a little skeptical. All I have done is tell my experiences the best I remember them. I have written the poetry as it came to my head. I never was an author or writer of any kind. I never cared for poetry, but I feel I was inspired to write some by my wonderful wife. With my final words, the time is 7:17. I still don't know what the 17 stands for, but it keeps appearing in my life very often.

Yesterday was two years since Marge passed on, and she let me know a couple times that she was doing fine. I was sitting at work reminiscing about the times I was grieving when my phone would ring one time. As I was thinking about that yesterday, my phone rang one time. A short time later, my radio started playing without me even turning it on. Think what you may, but to me these were all signals from Marge from the other side, telling me she is doing well in the afterlife.

The Beginning.

.